In You I live
Outside of You I'm nothing!

By: Rhonda Smith

In You I Live
Outside of You I'm nothing!
By. Rhonda Smith

First printing June 2010
Copyright Rhonda Smith. 2010
All rights reserved.

Library of Congress cataloging-in-publication-data
In You I Live/Rhonda Smith
ISBN: 978-0-615-37800-8

A Shuler Publications book
Published by Shuler Publications

Printed in the United States of America.

Cover Design: Melissa Shuler

Acknowledgments

To my Lover, my Strong Tower, my Refuge, my Protector, my Source, my Heart, my Rock, my Joy, my Peace, my Strength, my Helper, my Friend, my Husband, my Redeemer, my Healer, my Savior JESUS. You are my everything and I love you with all my heart, mind, soul, and strength. You are my life. Thank you Father God! I know I can never pay you back for all you have done for me. Thank you! Thank you Jesus your love is sweeter and sweeter everyday. I truly do love, to love you Lord! I love to worship and praise you. Please keep teaching me how to love you and how to receive your love.

Jada my love bug, my daughter, my Jesus girl, my princess. You are beautiful inside and out. I love you so much. I thank God for you. You have truly changed my life for the better. Thank you for being so patient with mommy! Greater works you will do! Greater works for the kingdom of God!

Jerrie and Kathy my mother and godmother all I can say is thank you. I love you ladies more than you will ever know. You have sown so much into me and your labor of love was not in vain!

Michael you are a great man of God and because of you I started going to New Birth in Lithonia, Georgia and you also taught me to be honest with God. Love you and thank you so much. You are a great blessing to the body of Christ.

Pastor Waid and Maxine Hobbs thank you thank

you thank you for being my spiritual mom and dad. Thank you for letting me use your laptop to type this book and thank you for letting me borrow your car to drive to work. I love you two so much. Thank you for loving me and my family. Thank you for believing in me. Thank you for pushing me into my destiny (smile). You two are a huge blessing to God's kingdom.

Bishop Eddie Long I never met you I've only shook your hand. Your ministry has and still is a great blessing to me. You are a huge blessing to the body of Christ. I miss New Birth! And because of your ministry I'm taking Authority for the kingdom of God!

Evangelist Genia Moss my best friend in the whole wide world. You are beautiful. You are passionate. You are HUGS!!! You are my sister and I truly thank God for you. You are a true example of a Proverbs 31 woman. Genia you taught me how to love. We met at T.D. Jakes Mega-fest in the A.T.L. And it was Jesus love at first sight. Thank you for believing in me. Thank you for praying and fasting with me. I love you more than you will ever know.

My editors Becky and Connie, thank you for all your love and support. You ladies are great gifts to the body of Christ.

Melissa and Curtis Shuler thank you so much for helping me with this book. You two are a great blessing to the kingdom of God. I'm grateful to have you two in my life.

Special thanks to my family and friends I love you so much. Thanks to TBN, Daystar, and Inspiration TV and to all the great and awesome pastors that have sown into my life through Christian TV. I love you and this book is for you All.   God bless you all.

IRON SHARPENETH IRON!

FORWARD

In You I Live" is a book of ups and downs. The author becomes quite transparent as she shares her life. Rhonda reveals the pit falls, the giants, and the addictions of her life; however she also recommends a way out of all of life's bondages. That way is asking Jesus into your heart. In the poems you will feel the pain and recognize the agony of growing up a poor black girl. The downward spiral, even though church is mentioned, takes Rhonda to places of entrapment that the enemy of her soul was leading to her demise. I have watched this young lady wrestle with life's problems over the last three years and I have seen her grow into a prayer warrior. No longer does she look back with the pain of the past since but she is moving forward and upward. Rhonda is allowing the past to propel her into a bright future because Jesus has become her every thing. Dear reader wherever you are on life's journey and no matter what life has sent your way, it is my opinion that this book will help guide you into a better way.

Waid Hobbs, Senior Pastor
Abundant Harvest Fellowship
Crescent City, Florida

Ye have not chosen me,
but I have chosen you,
and ordained you, that
ye should go and bring
forth fruit, that
whatsoever ye shall ask
of the Father in my name,
he may give it to you.
JOHN 15:16

Contents

Acknowledgments
Foreword
Wow!

WOW!

Wow! All I can say is wow! This book has been in the making for 18 years. I knew as a little girl, I would write a book. My intentions were all wrong. I wanted the fame and the wealth that I thought went along with writing a book. My mind wasn't right. I was a young foolish, angry girl from the South. I just wanted to move away from Florida and be free. I moved away to Georgia and I took the same mind set that I had in Florida. I now realize your way of thinking has to change before your situation will change. If you think on negative things then most likely you will have a negative life. Apostle Paul had to allow Jesus to change him from the inside outside, before God could use him. Healing can only take place internally. On the outside I had it going on. I had the material things and I kept myself up. But inside I was slowly dying. I wasn't happy with my life or the people within my life. I was a walking zombie that wore designer clothes. I would get up get high, drop Jada off to school and go to work high. Then get off from work pick up my daughter and go home and get high again. My life was a mess. I was trying to cover up hurt, shame, depression, unforgiveness, and anger.

After years and years of living away from Florida God sent me right back to Florida where it all started. God has mended old relationship. I have forgiven people from my past and started my life over again with a kingdom mindset. It's no longer what can Florida do for me it's now what could I do for Florida. How can I be a blessing to all the hurting people I see around my neighborhood. I no longer cared about the fame and the money. I cared about SOULS for God's kingdom. People are dying and going to hell daily. It's sad!

God is looking for vessels especially broken, vessels so He can heal them and fill them with his power (Holy Spirit) and send them out into the world to proclaim the truth in love. God wants to use people who will let their life be a testimony to His love and grace. I didn't just wake up with a willing heart I had to pray and fast for the desire to serve the Lord and His people. I had to really die to everything Rhonda wanted and thought (Phil. 1:21 for to me to live is Christ, and to die is gain). I know that dying to Rhonda, was the best thing that ever happen to me. God has filled me with so much courage, passion, and boldness. I don't care what people say about my relationship with Jesus. I don't care who stays or leaves.

Furthermore, I'm so honored that God has chosen me. After all the lying, cheating, fighting, and the stealing I had done. Wow! Father you still chose me. I feel like the most special woman in the world. Wow the God of heaven and earth wants to fill me with more of Him. I'm so glad that I have surrendered all my bad habits to God. I don't have a desire to go back and serve the devil. God has been so good to me and I just want to please my Daddy at all times. I want to bring a smile to His face everyday. I'm on a mission now, just like I gave the devil my all (when I was ignorant and trapped in sin) now I'm going to give my Lord and Savior Jesus Christ my all. I'm taking back souls for the kingdom of God.

Finally, here is my gift back to Jesus. I carried this

baby (my book) for years. And the devil almost stole it from me. I was delayed but not denied! God's word says when the enemy comes in like a flood the Lord will rise up a standard against him. Jesus had the book and I covered in His blood. Wow! This book is not mine it's a product of God's love, goodness, mercy, grace and forgiveness. I pray you find this gift to the kingdom of God a blessing to you. This book has truly been a blessing to me. I wouldn't trade this baby (the book) for anything. Lord, I thank you for the struggle, pain, disappointment, and the betrayals. I might have lost some people along the way. Through it all I'm a better person. I'm closer to Jesus then I was ever before. I hope I bring glory to your name Father God and I hope I continue to make You proud. *For a day in thy courts is better than a thousand. I had rather be a doorkeeper in the house of my God, than dwell in the tents of wicked. For the Lord God is a sun and shield: the Lord will give grace and glory: no good thing will he withhold from them that walk uprightly. O Lord of hosts, blessed is the man that trusteth in thee. Psalm 84:10-12*

1John 2:16 &17

For all that is in the world, the lust of the flesh, and the lust of the eyes, and the pride of life, is not of the Father, but is of the world. And the world passeth away, and the lust thereof: but he that doeth the will of God abideth forever.

Love Always Your Daughter

Rhonda

PAIN

He heals the broken hearted and binds up their wounds.
Psalm 147:3

The Beginning

When I first started writing poetry, I wrote it with an outside point of view. Plus I wrote through my pain. This habit I picked up in a small town call Satsuma Florida. Everything was outside. On the outside people would make comments about how nappy my hair was. They wouldn't say unique or different. They would turn their lips up and yell just nappy or nappy head. I'm glad I got over that! On the outside people made statements like your beautiful for a black, dark skin girl. No beautiful brown sugar or cocoa, mocha. Just black! The funny thing is most of the people that were putting me down was my very own family. The people I lived and ate with. They made a point of letting me know how dark I was just in case I had forgotten! Little did I know God had a plan to use my pain to heal people all over the world. Did I suffer from low self esteem yes! Did I fall into the arms of every man that made me feel special and beautiful yes!

Life in a small town was sad, painful, depressing, and lonely. People would put on a mask to hide the pain. They would put other people down to make themselves feel better. People would use their eyes and mouth never their heart. On the outside all I could see was dirt roads, railroad tracks, cornfields, racism, and bitter people. It really started to affect me to the point I changed. I once used my heart to see the world. But when I realized nobody cared then I changed my focus to my eyes. With my eye I saw how people got favor because of the color of their skin. With my eyes I saw hurt people hurt people. With my eyes I saw people being killed over money and drugs. I saw so much hatred and pain through my eyes. So I wrote about it. I had to express my anger and pain. I didn't want to use my mouth because my mother would always tell me your mouth is going to get you in trouble someday. I tried writing more than talking. I just couldn't ignore the racist teachers at my school. My mouth had got the best of me. People didn't like the fact that I told it like it was no holding back. In life people always say tell me the truth but when you do they get mad. I know how Jesus felt He was abuse and treated differently because He told the truth.

On the inside I was dying. I hated myself and everyone around me. How could my own family hurt me? How could people I didn't know me call me horrible names? I would always say I'm going to leave this town and make something of myself. I realize everything starts at home. If you don't kill the root of the problem then you will walk around carrying old baggage. I carried all my Satsuma baggage to Atlanta Ga. There I met other people that were carrying the same baggage. And wearing the same mask,   soon the load started getting to heavy. A lot of times I thought killing myself would have freed me from my load. I used drugs, people, and food to make me forget about my baggage, and I would visit church just to feel free. Soon as the service was over I found my baggage was still outside waiting for me.

My breaking point was on Super Bowl Sunday February 2005; I was getting ready for church. I went outside to start my car and it wouldn't start. I went back inside my apartment and cried. I was sick of my car, environment, and my life. I headed straight to the bathroom to smoke some weed and listen to Jay Z. I heard a voice say turn the radio on V103 gospel Sunday. I changed the radio station the music was just what I needed to hear. All I could do was cry. Then I started talking to God. And God started talking back. I couldn't believe God would talk to me because I was so high. I asked God was smoking weed a sin because I never read about it in the bible. God lead me to the front room where He told me to turn on the T.V. and it was on TBN, Paula White said "if you're doing something and you're not sure if it's a sin or not then it's a sin". At that point I flushed the weed down the toilet. And I cried out to Jesus like never before. Jesus changed my insides (my heart) and I haven't been the same. He washed the outside pain away.

For this people heart's is waxed gross, and their eyes are dull of hearing and their eyes they have closed: lest at any time they should see with their eyes, and hear with their ears and should see with their heart, and should be converted, and I should heal them. Matthew 13:15

Why I get mad

I get mad when I'm alone at night
I get mad when people have to die for what's right
I get mad because it's so hard to say goodbye
I get mad when I see homeless people on the street
I get mad when people don't have food to eat
I get mad when I read about black on black crime
I get mad because it happens all the time
I'm going to stop getting mad and help make a difference in this world
Because only dogs get mad

I dreamed a black dream

I dreamed a black dream last night

I tried to forget it with all my might

The dream stuck me deep down in my soul

It was about a black man strong and bold

He talked about things that black people were never told

That struck the white men down in their soul

The white men knew that the black man was telling his
people the truth

They wanted the black man to be stop

The white men called all his friends and even the crooked
cops

They put an end to the black man the night

You could smell burnt flesh all through the town

The black people knew that their leader wasn't around

The black people cried and asked God why a strong
black man must have to die

On the other hand the white men were filled with gleam

I hope I never have a black dream

My body cringes when I read this poem. I had so much hate and pain inside of me. I was very prejudice growing up. All I saw around me in the south was black and white. In high school I had to deal with prejudice teachers. I remember watching Roots and Mississippi burning and crying. I listening to older people talk about racism but I never really understood. There was time when I wanted to go play with other kids but my mother would tell me no. I grow up hearing the word Nigger and Cracker a lot. We had our church and they had their church. It was horrible no togetherness just hate.

As I got older my hatred for other races grew, I wrote this poem when I was still in grade school. It was around the time of the Rodney King beating, and I was angry. I just saw mad black people and mad white people. I wrote what I felt at the time. I thank God that he healed my mind and heart. I remember when God started working on me. It was when I moved to Atlanta and I came across white people that were really nice. I realize people are people no matter the color of their skin. God said we're made in His image. We're all God's children. God is love and the devil is hate. So since I'm made in the image of God I now choose to walk in love regardless of the color of someone skin.

Roman 12:10

Be kindly affectionate one to another with brotherly love; in honor preferring one another.

17TH BIRTHDAY

Happy birthday was a word I didn't hear no balloons,
cake, ice cream and no presents.

Just me sitting on the toilet crying.

Not a happy birthday from my daddy, best friend, aunts,
brother or sister, and not a word from my uncles

But I did get a special present from someone God.
(LIFE)!!!

Just a regular day no smile on my face

Birthdays are not that special to a poor black girl

Thank God for these 17 years!

Wow Rhonda you felt that bad? For many years I suffered from depression and suicidal thoughts. I thought my life was so boring. I felt my life would have been perfect if I had material things. The devil had me so confuse. By watching people on television, I had built my perfect life, full of presents, clothes, cars, and love.

All young girls want to know that they are special and on my 17th birthday I didn't feel loved or special. My father wasn't around and my mother was a single mother of three. Plus my mother took care of my great uncle and great grandmother, so she had a lot on her plate. She didn't have a relationship with God so she was dealing with her problems. She would work jobs here and there. But like most low income families we depended on government assistance and I hated it! I didn't like going to the grocery store with food stamps. I wanted my mom to have a steady job like my other friends parents. I remember getting so angry that I told her that I would never be like her. I wanted so much for my mother. My mom didn't have a car and we lived in a small town and the only jobs that were available were housekeeping jobs. I didn't like telling my friends that my mom cleaned people houses. My mom tried to do the best that she could. She made sure that we never went hungry.

My birthday was on the 26 at the end of the month and mama got her food stamps at the first of the month. We would always be down to peanut and jelly sandwiches at the end of the month. I didn't want a peanut butter and jelly sandwich with a candle stuck in it! Till this day I do not like peanut butter and jelly sandwiches, but my daughter Jada she loves them. Jada would rather have a peanut butter and jelly sandwich than a home cooked meal.

I'm glad my 17th birthday, is gone and in the past. It's now 2010 and I still haven't had an official birthday party nor do I even care. I'm so complete in Jesus that nothing else matters. One thing I do know when I get to Heaven I will have the best birthday party ever! I have learned to let go of the past and look forward to the future that God has for me.

I cry

As I sit here watching P.B.S tell the story of Martin Luther King's life I can't help but cry.

I cry for the man that walked in Jesus steps.

I cry for the man that only wanted to do his Father's will.

I cry for the man that wanted to help his fellow man.

I cry for the man, who just like Jesus died for his people.

I cry for the men that have forgotten about Martin Luther King.

I cry for the men that will never know his story.

I cry for the men that hang out on Auburn Ave selling drugs.

I cry for the women who walk up and down Auburn Ave. selling their bodies

I cry for the police officers that work right down the block.

I cry because just like Martin I have a dream that God will use me to bring change to a lost world.

I cry for the lady sitting on the corner of Auburn Ave. in her wheel chair asking for money.

I cry for the people that drive right pass her without a thought.

I cry for the people without compassion.

I cry out to God for the strength to keep doing His will.

I cry out for the true Warriors for Christ, who will give their life to do the Father's will no matter what.

I cry for the man that realize it doesn't matter

How long you live

It matters how you lived!

January 14, 2006

January 14, 2006 was a night like no other, I found myself watching TV. I watch a documentary on Martin Luther King's life, I had seen his life story before but this time it was so different. This documentary changed my heart. As I watch the show, all I could do was cry. I wonder where are the Martin Luther King's of my generation? And do they still remember his legacy. And do they remember what he stood for. I was caught up in the marches and the speeches that I forgot he was a true man of God. And he represented the kingdom of God. Martin was a warrior for Christ Jesus. He was our Moses!

Not shortly after I allowed Christ into my heart. A friend and I went to downtown Atlanta. As we walked down the street I saw so many lost souls. My heart went out to them and I asked God what I could do for his people. And the Holy Spirit said feed them. He said feed them food and feed them spiritual food. So I typed up a poem and added Bible verses; we made bag lunches that consisted of a sandwich, fruit and water. We loaded up the cars went downtown almost every Saturday. We handed out lunches and prayed for God's people. Soon we went from 30 lunches to 100 lunches and that's when I got familiar with Auburn Avenue. My heart went out to all the homeless people sleeping under the over pass. I couldn't believe that this street was the once famous Auburn Avenue! I wonder if Martin Luther King could have seen Auburn in 2006, how he would have felt. I felt so bad because the documentary showed Auburn when it was the place to be. Now all I could see was drug addicts, drug dealers, prostitutes, old abandon buildings, and homeless people.

I think God was getting me prepared for the road He had for me. Within months of feed the homeless I became one of them. I lost my apartment, my car, and my job within a 3 months span. But it didn't stop me! We still made the lunches and fed God's people. I was able to relate to them. My heart went out to them even more because I was in the same situation. Thank God that I wasn't on the street but I knew how it felt not to have a place of your own. Eventually we had to stop feeding the homeless and it was really hard because I made friends with so many people. And they were happy to see us on Saturday and I was happy to see them.

The experiences on Auburn Avenue change me forever and I still have a passion in my heart for the lost! I know how it feels to want to die. I know how it feels to lose everything like Job did in the Bible. I know how it feels to have your heart shattered in piece to the point you desire death over life. And I also know how it feels to receive love from strangers. Feeding the homeless wasn't about me! It was about showing the love of Jesus, which Martin Luther King did time and time again. I didn't realize at the time but we were walking in Jesus footsteps. Those people were thirsty for Jesus and His love.

Now I'm a teacher and I have little kids looking up to me. God has bless me to feed them knowledge and a double portion of love. I do miss and think about Auburn Avenue, but I have another generation that needs me. And I have to tell the story about Martin Luther King. I might not be able to talk about Jesus but I can tell them the story of Martin Luther King and his legacy. This book is my legacy to Jada and the next generation. My prayer is that God will give us the love and desire to make a difference in this world for Jesus not for ourselves. Only what we do for Jesus Christ will last!

I wore the mask

Monday morning I wore the confuse mask
I got up and went to a job that I hated

Tuesday I wore the materialistic mask
I brought a new pair of designer jeans trying to hid my
scars

Wednesday I wore the confident mask
I had on my confident skirt that day
I was confident that I would find a new job and boyfriend

Thursday I wore the dark child mask
My hair and nails weren't done
My clothes were old
I felt like a dark cloud was following over me

Friday I wore the just got paid mask
This mask helped me forget that I was living paycheck to
paycheck

Saturday I wore the no work today mask
This was my favorite mask
Because a lot of people had this mask too

Sunday I wore me but not for long!
I wore my scars and bruises to church
I fit right in
But soon I would go to the bathroom and slip on my
Sunday mask
This mask said I had it all together
It's hard to change when you're so use to hiding behind
different masks
My life is a lie and it's not complete
Because I still have to depend on wearing a mask all next
week!

Why I cry through my poetry

Crying through my poetry is therapy for me

Like Langston Hughes cried out disappointment
when he wrote: Dress up

Paul Dunbar cried out fear when he wrote: Sympathy

James Weldon cried out joy and happiness when he
wrote: Left every voice and sing

Countee Cullen cried out angry and turmoil when he
wrote: Sight

William Braithwaite cried out love when he wrote:
Sea Lyric

I cried out solitary when I wrote:

Why I cry through my poetry

His Life

I grew up hard
I played hard
I worked hard
I won hard

I listened hard
I studied hard
I loved hard
I fell hard
I ended up heart broken

Dedicated to Herman

I don't want to be here

I hate this situation I'm in
I don't want to be here in this mess
I should have went right but my emotion chose left
I want to be free from this dead situation
I'm getting tired of waiting
Yes I made a mistake I should have never said, "Yes"
When you told me no
Now I have to deal with this horrible decision
Should I stay or should I go

I don't want to be here it has nothing to do with the other person
I just want to be free
This situation has cause me so much pain and misery
I will never follow my heart
Because Father your word says, "you will know them by their fruit".
I went into this situation only thinking about me
I looked to someone to fill a void in me that they couldn't fill
And yes I'm angry and mad
I'm mad at myself for not waiting on God
I step out of your will

I should have guarded my heart

I don't want to be here
Please Father let this cup pass from me
Remove this thorn in my flesh
I promise that once you release me I won't get back into
this mess
So many lives have been hurt especially my daughter
All she ever wanted was a loving father
I have explained to her that people make mistakes
I told her to put her trust in Jesus and wait

I don't want to be here
I know God you can turn any situation around
I have forgiven and I have let go
I want to move forward
Jesus please here my cry
This is not fair
What did I do to deserve this?

So many times I have gotten myself into some very bad situations, because I didn't listen to God nor did I trust God. I whined and begged God to release me from the bad situations. One thing I can say in every bad situation that I got myself into, I always came out with more wisdom, power, and love for Jesus. No matter how bad things got, Jesus was always there with me. Sometimes I did feel alone in my situation. At those times I believed God was testing me. Maybe God wanted to see if I was going to try and do it myself or trust in Him. When I refused to put Jesus first in my life over husband, children, money, job, school, etc... I always failed.

Secondly, I learned my mistakes didn't just affect me but they affected my family and other people around me. I asked God for help, but when I didn't get the answer I wanted to hear then I made my own decision which ended up in failure. I had a problem surrendering to God's will. The bottom line is I didn't trust God's decision. Proverb 3:5 & 6 say, "Trust in the Lord with all your heart and lean not on your own understanding; in all your ways acknowledge Him (God) and He shall direct your paths." Anytime I tried to do something outside of God. I always failed, because outside of God I'm nothing. The Bible says, "In Him we live, and move, and have our being" Acts 17:28. The problem was I wanted to follow my heart and let my emotions lead me. The Bible says, "

The heart is deceitful above all things, and desperately wicked: who can know it." I made wrong decision because it felt good at the time and because my heart wanted me to. I learned not to trust my feelings or my heart. I had to choose to do what the word of God told me to do. I loved people even when they refused to love me. I surrendered my will to God. God's word says, "Love your enemies and pray for those who persecute you, that you may be sons of your Father in heaven." Matthew 5: 44 &45.

Lastly, if I would have never learned from my mistakes nor surrendered my will to God, I would have never written this book. God took me through some very bad situations and break my will. Jesus knew that once He changed me I would tell the world about it.

Broken

This pain has cut me deep
It has knocked me off my feet
It hurts to even sleep
Tears are the only way I can speak

Opening my mouth would only be death to me
I'm drowning in this pain
And it has gotten the best of me

My heart is frozen from this pain
Will I every smile again
I want to be free but when

My face is swollen from my tears
So much pain through out the years
I need help can anyone hear

Release me from this prison of death
I can't take it anymore
I'm losing my breath
I have nothing left

I'm so broken

That I can't even stand

I need someone to hold my hand

I hear a voice

"OPEN THE BOOK"

Open a book

No!

I don't want to read

Ok.

Where do I turn?

REVELATION 21:4-7

And God shall wipe away all tears from their eyes; and there shall be no more death, neither sorrow, nor crying, neither shall there be any more pain: for the former things are passed away.

And he that sat upon the throne said, Behold, I make all things new. And he said unto me, Write: for these words are true and faithful.

And he said unto me, it is done. I am Alpha and Omega, the beginning and the end. I will give unto him that is athirst of the fountain of the water of life freely.

He that overcomes shall inherit all things; and I will be his God, and he shall be my son.

So if I overcome all this mess

I will inherit You and be bless

What!

I have lost everything, hopes, dreams, and people too

"IT DOESN'T MATTER WHAT HAS HAPPEN TO
YOU
I MAKE ALL THINGS NEW!"

Dedicated to Pastor Paula White
Church without Walls in Tampa Florida

My worst days were my best days!

My two worst situations were when I ended up homeless and I almost lost custody of my daughter. I ended up homeless because once again I made some really stupid choices. I allowed pride to get in the way. I didn't want to humble myself and ask for help. At that time I was thinking about myself. And because I was being selfish and prideful, I almost lost custody of my daughter. I remember the pain like it was yesterday, Jada and I had no place to stay so we slept on a couch at my job in Atlanta Georgia. Wow! I wanted to die. I felt like I had no way out. I prayed and asked God to help me and He did. Through that difficult time I learned how to trust God. I realized my strength came from the Lord and not from me. God eventually bless us with a place to stay.

When I thought things couldn't get worst, my sister died and then I got a letter from the courthouse. They wanted me to appear in court to fight over custody for Jada. I remember sitting in the courthouse and listening to all the lies that were said about me. The truth was I lost my apartment but I wasn't and unfit mother. I remember going to the bathroom in the courthouse and crying. I couldn't believe that this was happening to me. I felt like a loser. I wanted to crawl in a hole and die. I knew I was a good mom. But the facts said something different. And right then the court was looking at the facts but my Jesus was looking at the truth. I had no lawyer so I had to defend myself. Through it all I learned to trust God. The court case lasted for almost 3 years; I was back and forth to court. I felt weak and I wanted to give up. The bible says in 2 Corinthians 12:9 my grace is sufficient for you, for my power is made perfect in weakness. Each time I walked in that courtroom, Jesus was there giving me power to get through it. Did I feel the power no. Did I see the power no. I just knew when people told me to give up, or just giving Jada away. I said "no". I knew Jada was a blessing to me and I knew the devil wanted to steal my blessing.

On the last and finally day of court I was scared. I keep tell myself just trust God, just trust God. The Guard of Lien said "We can't take her daughter because Rhonda is a good mother". All I could do was praise God, because for 3 years I had tried to tell the courts that I was a good mother!

I can now say like Paul did in 2 Corinthians 12:10, I delight in weakness, in insults, in hardships, in persecution, in difficulties. For when I am weak, then I am strong. Now when people come to me for advice with custody cases I can tell them my testimony and let them know there is no problem or bad situation God can't fix!

Furthermore, I took accountability for my action. Once I did that it opened the door for Jesus to change me. I confessed my sins and my mistakes to the Lord. I couldn't hide behind my pride anymore and I had to make decision based on my daughters well being. Jesus also taught me about forgiveness during those 3 years. God gave me the power to forgive everyone that was involved in the court case. I also learned that you will reap what you sow (Galatians 6:7). The bottom line is I hurt a lot of people in my past and even though God forgave me. I still had to reap the repercussion of my action. I now sow love, mercy, honest and peace so that I can reap love, mercy, honest and peace back.

To God be the glory forever and ever!

FORGIVENESS

Forgive, and you will be forgiven

Luke 6:37

I choose

I choose today to live a life with purpose

I choose to forgive you and set you free

I choose to let go of all the hurtful things you did to me

I choose to no longer seek vengeance upon you

I choose to receive forgiveness for my sins

I choose to allow God to heal me for my wrongs

I choose to not judge you

I choose to pray for you

I choose to bless you

This day I choose to no longer be the victim.

I choose to love you with the love of Christ

This poem is dedicated to all the people I hurt. I'm sorry!

Forgiveness

This is a toughie! So may people suffer through unforgiveness and I was one. My struggle started in my childhood with my family. From childhood to teen years it carried into my adulthood and it almost killed me. I never dealt with it, but it dealt me for years. I didn't know what to do. Yes, I did say I'm sorry or I forgive you but I never did. I always waited for the opportunity to seek vengeance. Until I allowed Jesus to rule and reign in my life, then God started peeling me like a thick onion and yes like peeling an onion I cried, because it wasn't easy. I never really wanted to forgive because I didn't know how to. So I cut people loose and moved on with no thought about it.

One day it got so bad and God kept throwing unforgiveness in my face. I went into my prayer closet and He took me back to my childhood. He showed me my family and all the things they did and things I did to them. He showed me the hatred, anger, pain, and bitterness that were standing in the way of forgiveness. There is always a reason why you won't forgive. That day I cried out to God and gave it all to Him. I forgave my family and all the other people that hurt me. After that I received Gods forgiveness for my sins. It's a sin when you have unforgiveness in your heart. If the unforgivness stay in your heart to long it can kill you. Yes, I hurt people. Hurt people will hurt other people. I wanted to believe that God would forgive me, and that day I did. Now did I feel, different? No! But I knew change had taken place in me. Did I still think about the hurtful situations? Yes! I no longer wanted to seek vengeance or play the victim role. I got up and brushed myself off. I went deeper in the Lord.

God takes unforgiveness and forgiveness very serious, because He loves us so much that He sent his Son to die for us. When you receive Jesus Christ into your heart and ask for forgiveness He immediately forgives us of all our sins. Yes! He forgives every one no matter how big or small. He totally forgets about it and we start afresh. So just like God we have to forgive as well. Does it mean that we have to allow those same people to hurt us again? NO! God wants us to forgive them. So we can release them from our lives. I allowed unforgiveness in my relationships and my marriage. Unforgiveness is like a deadly disease that poisons everybody it touches. And yes it can kill you! If you let it. The devil will tell you that you're weak and a loser for letting them off the hook. God's word says, "Do not repay anyone evil for evil. Be careful to do what is right in the eyes of everybody. If it is possible, as far as it depends on you, live at peace with everyone. Do not take revenge, my friends, but leave room for God's wrath, for it is written: It is mine to avenge and repay Romans 12:17-19". Nobody goes unpunished.

My most painful example with unforgiveness was when my sister died. My sister and I fought like all other sisters. And I know she really loved me. She just had a strange way of showing it. For so many years I carried pain and angry in my heart towards her. I always kept my distance from her. I found out that my sister received Christ and that she was different. I went to see her and I didn't see a difference because she still said hurtful things to me. I build up a wall and cut her off. One thing you have to realize with salvation it is a process. God can totally deliver and change a person over night and sometimes He doesn't. I wasn't serving God at the time so I didn't know this.

Years went by and my sister gave birth to her last baby and she got sick. So I went to see her again. I didn't know that it would be the last time I would ever see her alive. Now on that day she was different she was so nice to me. I couldn't believe it. I have to admit I wasn't nice back. I kept thinking about the past. My heart went out to her a little because she looked like death. After that I went on with my life and I remember talking to my best friend Genia. And Genia suggested I go spend time with my sister. I agreed to please Genia but I never follow through.

In April I had to go to court in Georgia. I didn't want to go. I didn't have peace about the trip. So I left on a Friday afternoon. On Saturday, my friends and I went shopping and had dinner, we had so much fun. Saturday night I couldn't sleep. I started feeling sad and depress. I couldn't explain my feelings. I started praying to Jesus. I still felt bad. So I got my pen and pad. I started writing a poem about death, fear, confusion, and love. I titled the poem (In the shadow of death). The poem was as if someone was dying but they were afraid. It's was like the person wanted to die then the person was confuse. Saturday night ran into early Sunday morning. I finally went to sleep for a few hours. I got back up to go to early morning church service at New birth. I still didn't feel right but I pressed on to church. Once I got to church I started worshiping Jesus and singing His praises.

Then something lifted off me, I felt so free. I said to myself when I get back home I was going to write a poem and call it (I'm free).

Shortly after, my cell phone started vibrating while I was in church I thought it was strange. I looked at the number and it was my mother and she had called me more than once. I was going to leave in the middle of service to call her but the Holy Spirit said no. So I stayed in church and had a wonderful time. Once service was over I went to my car. I checked my messages and I had an urgent message from my godmother. I started praying. I called my godmother and she told me that my sister had died early Sunday morning. My body went dead. All I could do was scream and cry. I was so hurt.

After the funeral, I was sad and angry. I was angry at God and I was angry at my sister. I had a horrible pain inside my heart every time I thought about my sister. I didn't know what it was until my friend Ekeias told me that it was unforgiveness. He told me that I needed to forgive my sister and release her. I was like how, she's dead. He told me to write her a letter and tell her everything. He told me not to hold back. And then he said read the letter out loud to Jesus and burn it. To be honest a part of me wanted to forgive her and let go; then a part of me wanted to hold on to the pain so I could keep playing the victim role. I knew if I had forgiven her then I could no longer hide behind the pain and blame her.

On a cold night, I got fed up with the pain and hurt. And I prayed and asked Jesus to give me the power to write the letter. And Jesus did, so I wrote the letter. I listed all the bad things my sister did to me. And I listed all the bad things that I had done to her. Then I went outside and read it aloud then I burned it. I ended the letter to my sister with I forgive you. After that night the pain was gone and I was free. I realized my battle was not with my sister but the devil. The devil used my sister to hurt me. The devil also used me to hurt my sister. God's word says, "We wrestle not with flesh and blood, but against principalities, against powers, against the rulers of the darkness" Ephesians 6:12.

The Bible says "The thief comes only to steal and kill and destroy" John 10:10. I had allowed the devil to steal my relationship with my sister. He was trying to kill me with unforgiveness. I'm glad Jesus gave me victory over unforgiveness and the devil. Jesus paid the price for all my sins. I just had to be honest with Jesus and tell Him how I felt and He healed my heart.

And Jesus can do the same for you. If you don't believe me then try it. I promise that your life will never be the same.

I'm no longer a victim

I'm no longer a victim of my past
I have let it all go and I'm free at last
I'm no longer a victim to all the lies the enemy told me
I have the Word of God and God's truth has set me free
I'm no longer a victim to betrayal, disappointments, and
rejection from people I loved

You see so much has happen to me
Since I surrender my all to Jesus Christ I'm free
Free from pain, free from opinions, free from drama, and
free from myself
In Jesus there is love, peace, joy, and health

Please don't feel sorry for me
I'm trusting in my Savior and doing work for His
kingdom
And because of this I'm no longer a victim

Dedicated to Curtis Shuler, Derrick Gilyard, and other
men and women in jail and prison, keep doing the will of
God. You are not forgotten!

Thank you

This is to all the people that made my life great
You thought you could break me and make me
lose hope
People like you kept me a float

You thought you could trap me and make me give up
People like you motivated me to keep my head up

You thought you could kill my dreams and me stop
People like you inspired me to make it to the top

Matthews 5:44 But I say unto you, love your enemies,
bless them that curse you, do good to them that hate you.

DELIVERANCE

And the Lord saved them by a great deliverance. 1 Chronicles 11:4

I'm Free

I'm free to love

I'm free to be who God created me to be

I'm free to praise Jesus

I'm free to laugh

I'm free to watch my children grow

I'm free to love Jesus

I'm free to walk in my destiny

I'm free to leave so please do not cry or mourn my leaving

This is the way it had to be

I have fulfill my purpose and my destiny

Now it's just my Savior and me

Thank you Jesus that now I'm free!

Dedicated to my sister Melanie

Process

I grew up mad at the world
In my heart I wanted to be loved

I smoked weed
In my heart I wanted to stop

I used people for my on gain
In my heart I wanted to help them

I grew up reading the Bible and going to church
What happen where did I go wrong?
So I called out to Jesus and He heard my cry
He said, "I will change you and get you out of this mess
but first you have to realize it' a process"

This is one of my favorite poems. All my life I heard about God. We had a church in our backyard. Going to church and reading the Bible was the norm. Nobody ever sat down and told me about Jesus. All I knew is that you had to go to church, pray, and receive Jesus Christ as your Lord and Savior. I asked Jesus into my heart at a young age. Once I decided to do good and not evil, my world changed. The enemy (the devil) started attacking my life through my family and strangers. I felt like an outcast. I couldn't take anymore. So I went from toting a bible to hating everybody and myself. I felt like I had failed God. I felt like He didn't love me anymore. I was so wrong and I wanted so bad to live for the Lord. I wanted to be like my great grandmother. My great grandmother Mary Wilson was a true woman of God. My grand mother would walk to the next city to go to church because we didn't have one in our town. My great grandfather her husband wouldn't take my grandmother to church. Grandmother didn't have a license so after church she would get a ride with someone from church. Until one day God answered her prayers. My great grandfather and her sons built her a nice big church in her backyard. We had a path from the back door of our house to the church. You couldn't run from church and if you were sick someone would carry you to church. I still remember the smell in our church. It smelled like fresh olive oil.

After my great grandmother died, the church past away with her and something died in all of us when she died. My mother didn't go to church so she never made us. I didn't have a father to make me. I don't really remember when I went back to the world's way of life but I did. I did everything the bible told me not to do. First I started having sex, smoking weed, and then hanging around all the wrong people. Deep down inside I knew it was wrong but I just didn't know how to stop. When I thought I was pregnant I would throw up a quick prayer to heaven asking God to please save me. I would always promise to change and go to church but as soon as my cycle would come I was back in the streets. I know God knew I was lying. Wow! God I thank you for your grace. I should have died in my sin and went to hell. I'm so glad Jesus never gave up on me. I truly believe I'm only here because of my praying grandmother. God's word says, "The prayers of the righteous avail if much".

Finally out of nowhere my life started to go down hill. I got sick of guys, using drugs stopped being fun, and I got tired of the clubs. I decided to give up. I felt in my heart that God was drawing me back to him. I could only fight and run for so long. I would have had a better chance fighting a lion. God won the battle and my heart. God welcomed me back with open arms. For once I felt safe, loved, and free. I finally realized the scripture didn't lie. God's word says "If you raise a child in the way he needs to go. He might stray but they will soon come back". Please teach your children about Jesus and teach your children how to have a personal relationship with Jesus.

I soon found out there are two wills, God's will or my will. My will was sex, drugs, men, and death. I will never forget when I cried out to God with all my heart. I had to say not my will God but Your will be done. God went to work. Jesus gave me the power to ditch the drugs, clubs, and everything else that wasn't His will for my life. God had a plan and a purpose for me. God's word declares this over our life "Before I formed you in the womb I knew you, before you were born I set you apart I appointed you as a prophet to the nations" Wow! My Father God knew that I was going to write this book and proclaim His goodness, faithfulness, mercy, power, and grace. The devil wanted to kill me before time like he has done with so many other people. This all brings me back to the day I was going through my old journals. I read about all the men and other things I had done. I came a across this letter that I wrote to God asking Him to kill me in my sleep. I also wrote letters asking God to help me and change me. At that moment the Holy Spirit spoke and said PROCESS. Thank you Heavenly Father for processing me. God knew about all my failures, addiction, and stupid mistakes. God never changed His mind about me. He still used me to do His will. Man would have told me no. They would have said you're a single mother, you didn't finish college, but God said yes I will use you Rhonda! I will send my Son Jesus to die for you and cover all your sins. And I will send great men and women of God into your life to help you learn more about me. God said I'm going to change your desires and give you my Godly desire. God said I will love you so much that you will not want to sin anymore Rhonda. And even if you fall I will give you the boldness to come to me (Father God) and ask forgiveness and I will forgive you! Wow! I feel like the most special woman in the world my God, my Daddy, my Jesus did all that work for me. The only thing I did was BELIEVE! I made a decision to believe all the wonderful things my grandmother used to say about God. I made a decision to believe that He was my healer, my redeemer, my savior, my comforter, my provider, my peace, my joy, and my friend! *And in all the land, says the Lord, two thirds shall be cut off and perish, but one third shall be left alive. And I will bring the third part through the fire, and will refine them as silver is refined and will test them as gold is tested. They will call on my name, and I will hear and answer them. I will say it is my people; and they will say, the Lord is my God. Zechariah (amp) Chapter 13:8 & 9*

Defeated

You are defeated, you fierce giant in my life

Yes I was scared at first of you

But I soon realize I had Christ and there was nothing you could do

Giant you talked a good talk and walked a good walk

Yes I was afraid because I listen to your lies

The Holy Spirit gave me wisdom, knowledge, and revelation and the scales fell from my eyes

Now here is the truth: you tried to stop me from reaching my destiny

I had to kill you before you killed me!

With Jesus on my side I knew I could beat it

Now you no longer rule and reign over my life you are defeated

1 Samuel 17:9

If he be able to fight with me, and kill me, then will we be your servants: but if I prevail against him, and kill him, then shall ye be out servants, and serve us.

Giants come in every shape, color, and size. They are not your friends, just a device that the devil tries to use to stop you from accomplishing your destiny. I had plenty in my life. I thought that once you received Christ all of it would go away. But that's just the beginning. Once you receive the power from Jesus, the devil is mad now and he will do any and everything to stop you. He will even use your family, friends, kids, sex; drugs, food and the list goes on and on. But you have to remember the bible says, you can do all things through Christ which strengthens you. You alone can't defeat a giant you have to use Jesus. Jesus died for every giant that you are facing or will face. He defeated them before we were even born. So He knows what to do. We have to make a decision to live a righteous life through Christ Jesus. God will tell you and give you a strategy plan for battle. The most important thing to do before battle is to listen to God and never go to battle without Jesus.

Here is my testimony of how God defeat a giant in my life. When I was young I lived in a country town with only one traffic light, no fun and nothing to do. People turned to drugs for entertainment. So I tried smoking weed as a teenager but never like it. I later learned that my dad struggled with this same giant. Moving right alone, When I left home I went to college and made friends with people that smoked weed. So I tried it again. I still didn't like it, but it took my mind off my problems for awhile and then once the high was gone. I was back stuck with the same problems. I didn't realize that I was destroying my brain cells plus feeding demonic spirits. The more I smoke weed, the more power I gave the demonic spirits. The demonic spirits control you.

That's why people who do drugs either eat a lot or not at all, or sleep a lot or don't sleep at all or have sex a lot or not at all. The bottom line is it all leads to Death. The demonic spirits will tell you to kill yourself or kill others, it will tell you lie upon lie until you defeat the demonic spirits or they will destroy you.

So after teen years, college years, and motherhood I found myself right back smoking weed and this time I like it. But once I found out I was pregnant I stop until my daughter was born. After I had my baby girl my life changed. I couldn't really party or hang out much so I got depressed and started smoking again. I knew it was wrong I wanted to stop. I prayed and asked God to take it away. But each time I did pray someone would always come and give me some free weed. All through this I was still going to church and smoking weed after church.

Until one day, I will never forget it was Super Bowl Sunday. I had it all planned out I was going to go to church come home smoke weed, eat, and watch the Patriots win the Super Bowl. I got Jada and I dressed and got into my car to head off to church and my car wouldn't start. I was so hurt because I really wanted to go to church. So I could feel better and then go back home not changed. You see I was addicted to church but not addicted to Jesus. And there is a difference. People say, "I'm in the church". But is the church in you. The devil goes to church! So back to my life, I couldn't go get my quick Sunday morning church fix. My neighbor came out and told me to go inside and have church. So I went into my house rolled up a joint (because I didn't have a blunt) and turned on Jay Z the Black album and had church! The more I listen to music about drugs the more I wanted them. For some strange reason I started talking to God. And God started talking back to me. Now it wasn't a loud voice with thunder and lightning. Just a nice still voice in my heart, I know you're saying how I know the difference between God and the devil's voice. Well I grew up in the church; we had a path from the back door of our house to the church. And I received Christ at a young age and The Holy Spirit would talk to me. You will never forget your daddy's voice.

Therefore I asked God if He talked to people when their high and He said, "yes." Well since I had God's attention I asked Him if smoking weed was a sin and if it is why it isn't in the bible. He told me to go turn on the T.V. to TBN and there was this preacher name Paula White and she said if you're doing something and it seem like a sin but you don't know then it is a sin. I immediately flushed my weed down the toilet and set on my couch and cried out to the Lord like never before. And Jesus changed my heart and life forever. Now was everything sweet and peaceful no. The Holy Spirit showed me in a dream that one of my ex boyfriend was going to come over and bring me some weed. And it happened the same day. I didn't give in I told him no. My battle had started and the devil was mad. I said if Jesus did it before He will do it again. Jesus told me to stop hanging around people that smoked weed and before I could do that news got around to my friends that I had quit smoking weed so a lot of them stop hanging around me. Jesus made it easy for me.

Now that Jesus has delivered me from the bondage of weed now I can go talk to people that smoke weed and not be tempted. I can even smell weed smoke and not have a desire for it. I have a new desire and it's Jesus! He is the lover of my soul. He is my life! And He defeated my giant for me. Jesus gave me the power to say no and He will give you the same power. I'm so bless that I can share my testimony with the world. Jesus brought me out. My giant didn't kill me.

While I was writing this essay for my book, my mother told me that the police found this famous D.J. dead in his apartment from a overdose of drugs. I pray as you read this book that you will take this battle seriously. The devil wants to kill us! I pray you will receive Christ and live!

What did I gain?

I gave up my dreams for you what did I gain?

I gave up my self-esteem for you what did I gain?

I gave up my love for you what did I gain?

I gave up the most important thing for you what did I gain?

I gave up my heart for you what did I gain?

I gave up my joy for you what I did gain?

I gave up my body for you what did I gain?

I gave up my family for you what did I gain?

I gave up my time for you what did I gain?

At the end of my poem I gave you up!

And I gain so much love and peace through my pain.

I gain back all my love and joy two things you couldn't contain.

Thank you for teaching me a valuable lesson losing you was the greatest blessing!

Dedicated to my cousin Tasha G.

Yesterday I died

Yesterday I died and it felt so good
I died to all the old hurt and pain that plagued me for many
years
I died to every lie that was told about me
I died to every person that ever hurt me
I died to low self-esteem
I died to ignorance
I died to prejudice
I died to the fear of the unknown
I died to addiction to food and drugs
I died to every lie that was told to me
I died to all the people I hurt

Today I live
Today I live with joy
Today I live with high self-esteem
Today I live with victory
Today I live with love for myself
Today I live with wisdom
Today I live with love for others
Today I live with love for Jesus
Today I live my life
Today I live the new Rhonda

Matt. 10:39 He that find his life shall lose it: and he that lose
his life for my sake shall find it

My favorite scripture is Philippians 1:21 (For me to live is Christ, and to die is gain). I want to live in Christ all the way, not when things are going good. No I want to serve Jesus and suffer with my Lord. When we die to flesh it hurt sometimes. Especially when we die to our flesh (sin) and man nature, (emotions, evil desire, and evil thoughts), I know from the scripture in Philippians when I allow God to consume me, then God will take pleasure in filling me with more of Him. We need to be hungry for the things of the Lord. We need to seek His face. Are we really hungry today or are we just satisfy with same old same old. I was happy with going to church and praying for my family. I had material things plus I was saved and on my way to Heaven. I felt sad when I saw other people on there way to Hell. God let me fill His pain for His children. It's so sad we have so many Christian in this world and we refuse to open our mouth and tell someone the good news about Jesus Christ dying for all of our sins and then rising from the dead. We have to get over ourselves! It's truly not about us; it's about God's children hearing the gospel at any cost. It's about loving God's children to Jesus. Notice I said loving, we have to show love and compassion to God's children. If we are having problems with our love walk then we must ask Jesus to fill us with his love.

Wow! How can we not tell people about the goodness of Jesus, because most of us are still walking in sin? We are still going to church then smoking weed, cheating on our spouses, lying etc…How can we lead someone to Christian and we haven't really surrender to Christ ourselves! It's time out for playing church it's time for us to be the church and rise up. It's time for us to cry out to God for holiness. We must get sick of our sins. Christ can't shine in our life if we're covered with sin. Jesus sees what we're doing behind closed doors. Let's be real with Jesus and tell Him about our struggles cry out to Him until He breaks our will. Jesus asked God to take this cup from Him in the garden. He kept praying until He surrender and His will was broken, that's why He said, "Not my will but Your will be done" Can we say that today? Lord I want Your will or are we still playing games with the devil! God's word says "I know thy works, that you are neither cold or hot: I would you were cold or hot. So then because you are lukewarm, and neither cold or hot, I will vomit you out of my mouth". Wow! God is not talking to a sinner man He is talking to His church His bride. We can't have one leg in the world and one leg in the church. We are either for the devil or God. There is no in between!

We fail as Christians when we try to live a life outside of Jesus. I'm totally lost without Him. Jesus is my everything, I have to ask God daily to help me to not sin against Him. We live in a sinful world. The devil is out to kill, steal, and destroy us. We have to trust and rely on our Rock Jesus. We have to ask the Holy Spirit to fill us with His power, wisdom, understanding, and knowledge. We have to allow the Holy Spirit to lead us into all Truth. God's word is the Truth. We get caught up in facts but Jesus is the Truth and the way to eternal life.

Lastly I wrote this book to give God all the glory. He is a good God and beside Him there is no other. God has a great destiny for you. Just by you reading this book, let's me know God is not finish with you. God wants you to live for Him. He wants you to accept Jesus Christ as your Lord and Savior. He wants you to be a witness of His mercy, grace, and power. He wants you to surrender your all to Him!

So called friends

Friends said he wouldn't change. And I was wasting my time, but God told me to pray and be obedient and he would be mine.

Friends said he doesn't love you and you need to leave him alone, but God said stay faithful and I will bring him back home.

Friends said he would use you and mistreat you, but God said put your trust in me. I will make him love you until eternity.

Friends said he would abandon you and your child, but God said hold on I will make him change it might take awhile.

Friends said aren't you tired of him walking out on you, but God said he will return because I will let him see Jesus Christ in you.

Friends said he love the street life. And love for Jesus Christ he lacked, but God said love him and forgive him. I will humble him and show him that you always had his back.

The point is I love this man and God knew my feelings were true, but the devil didn't want me happy that's why he used so called friends like you. To say mean things and make me lose hope, but God said yes. I know his answer is true. That's why I no longer listen or hang around so-called friends like you!

Today I decided to stand

I lost my job
I thought I was going to lose my mind
I decided to stand

My car broke down
I thought I was going to lose my mind
I decided to stand

I got pregnant and became a single mother
I thought I was going to lose my mind
I decided to stand

Someone I thought would always be there for me walked
out on me
I thought I was going to lose my mind
I decided to stand
Now I'm raising my daughter without a car
And no job
Living in a shelter
After all this happen
I thought for sure I was going to lose my mind
So I called on the name of Jesus and He held my hand
Jesus gave me the strength that allowed me to stand

4/20/06

Stand

You come to a point when you have to stand for something or you will fall like rain! People said I had hit rock bottom. I thought my life was over, little did I know this was just the beginning of my life. I learned to stand without the material things that I thought I needed. I thought I would die without my car. No I just learned how to ride the bus until God blessed me with another car. My biggest fear was to become homeless and be a single parent. I felt like Job. Yes I made mistakes but God turned all my mistakes around and made me better not bitter. I learned how to trust and stand on God's word. There's nothing I can't do. I realize when you have nothing, no friends, no money, and no home. You will always have Jesus. Once you know that then you can stand!

I use to love hip hop

I use to love hip hop but I realize hip hop didn't love me

Hip hop told me who I was going to be

It told me that I was a shorty, no I'm more like a tally being 5"10 and all

Hip hop told me to get high ride till I die

No I rather get high off Jesus and ride straight to Heaven

Hip hop told me I was a ghetto girl, drama queen, and other things I rather not say

Hip hop never told me I was made in the imagine of God

Hip hop told me to sell drugs, turn tricks, and shaker my money maker

Hip hop never told me to seek wisdom and seek God's destiny for my life

Hip hop told me I was pretty if I had big legs, long hair, and a big booty

Hip hop never said that beauty starts in the inside

Hip hop never told me that Jesus love is what makes me beautiful

I no longer look for love

In music lyrics made up by some people who don't even know what love is

Jesus Christ is love

Jesus Christ is the true Ride or Die Soldier and His love will never stop. And this why I no longer love hip hop!

I want your company

I want you to be where I'm at

But you decided to take the road that leads to
regret

Every time I think of you my heart gets upset

I want you to go where I'm going

But you decided to take the street that leads to pain
and defeat

I think of you and my heart gets weak

I want you to grow

But you decided to take the path that leads to no
hope

I think of you and my heart gropes

I want you to see

But you decided to walk the path, rundown the
road, and joggle down the street blindfolded

Eyes hidden in a world of deceit

I think of you and my heart can't speak

So I go on my journey alone

Praying that God will lead you back home

Sometimes we want people to travel down our road. Eat what we eat. Laugh at our jokes. But sometimes we have to go at it alone. Before I gave my life to Christ, no let me change that. Before I asked Jesus to come into my heart, I had lots of friends that I thought loved me for me. But once I stopped going to the clubs, smoking weed, and partying. I found myself alone. God was calling me out from among my friends. Jesus was taking me to another level in Him. At first, it hurt but I soon got over the loneliness, pain, and rejection. I felt like my friends were rejecting me but it wasn't me. They were rejecting the Christ in me. Darkness will always run from light. For example when you go into a dark room and turn on the lights darkness has to flee.

God wanted to see if I was going to choose me friends over Jesus. I was at a crossroad. Keep my friends and stay in sin and end up in hell. Or leave my friends move forward and choose a life with Jesus. I had to really pray and ask God to give me the power to let go. And Jesus gave me the power and now God has blessed me with new friends. They truly do love me for me. I learned a valuable lesson through letting go. Whatever you give up for Christ, God will bless you with double and you will have no regrets. When you ask Jesus to be your Savior, you might have to give up some people but God will bless you with so much more. Never try to change people. You just keep doing what God has called you to do and Move Forward!

1 Corinthians 15:33 do not be misled: "Bad company corrupts good character."

1 Psalms 1:1-3 blessed is the man who does not walk in the counsel of the wicked or stand in the way of sinners or sit in the seat of mockers.

But his delight is in the law of the Lord, and on his law he meditates day and night. He is like a tree planted by streams of water which yields its fruit in season and whose leaf does not wither. Whatever he does prospers.

This poem is for the colored girls who lived at the end of the rainbow and made it!

You said I wouldn't be anything
I lived in a rat-infested apartment building
I lived without running water and no lights
I lived off peanut butter and jelly sandwiches
I lived with all my kids and no baby daddy
I lived standing in a long welfare line
I lived washing clothes and floors for other people
I lived picking cotton
I lived wanting someone to love and hold me but I couldn't find anybody
I lived listening to people tell me how ugly and black I was
I lived crying for a way out
I lived dreaming for a way out
I lived reading books about women that went through the same thing I did and didn't make it
I lived learning that I was special
I lived having faith in God
I lived knowing nothing is impossible if you trust in Jesus Christ and this why I truly made it!

Dedicated to all the women that grew up hard and found out there wasn't a pot of gold at the end of the rainbow. We found something better Jesus! He is better than all the gold in the world!

We made it! I will never forget reading the book about colored girls at the end of the rainbow. I was young and living at home. I felt their pain. Wow I thought they had horrible lives. I never wanted my life to end up like that. As I got older I forgot about the book and the colored girls. Now I was one of those girls living at the end of my rainbow. Where was my pot of gold? Instead of finding a pot of gold, I had to fight for my gold. I thought I could find it in drugs, food, sex, and clothes. The pot of gold was me. No one ever told me that, I thought I was ugly, fat, and stupid. Little did I know that I was a gold mine! Before I was formed in my mother's womb, God put His Spirit in me. I realized if you don't know what you have then you will allow people to steal what you got. I allowed food to steal my waistline. I allowed men to steal my self-esteem. I allowed drugs to steal my mind. But not for long, as I looked in the mirror of my soul, I looked pass the weave, makeup, and pain. There it was me! Yes me! The beautiful woman God made me to be, the writer, friend, mother and helper. Many times I would look in the mirror and see nothing. But not this time, it was different. I had to do a double take, Rhonda you are beautiful I said out loud. I said girl your skin is glowing. No makeup just my skin. For once I saw the sweet intelligent person that I so loved. She smiled back at me. Its ok I won't hurt you. I had spent so many years trying to hurt myself. I tried to kill myself with things and people. My soul screamed Rhonda you made it! Your still here, yeah I'm still here. As tears filled my eyes, I thought about all the women that traveled the road I did but didn't make it. I'm still here, echoed through my mind! The funny thing here wasn't a house, car, man, food, or a job. Here was peace with myself. Here was joy with myself. Here I was able to stand after wanting to die. Here I was happy to be alive. Here I was free! I found my pot of gold salvation through Christ Jesus!

I know I have been changed

My
My
Life is sweet life is grand
My Lord and Savior holds my life in his hands
And it feels good words can't describe just how good it is

I know I have been changed
I didn't wake up from birth with this feeling ya'll
No! No!
My life was rough and very very tough
I had some sleepless night and plenty of fights
But through it all
I know I been changed

My smile is brighter and I laugh louder
My soul feels so much better
It feels good to be different and still understood
I know I have been changed

Listen and listen close to these words I'm going to boast
Are you listening can you hear me
Not with your ears but your heart
The world didn't changed me ya'll

You know what made my heart sing
And what made me want to live again
JESUS!!
Yes Jesus
I know I been changed

I no longer mess around
I love my Jesus because
I'm His rose
I'm special in his eyes
No longer having to wear a disguise
I don't care if I'm not beautiful in your eyes
Listen and listen close
Not with your ears but your heart
I want to tell you
What Jesus told me last night?
That made me feel just right
He said "Rhonda I knew you before you were in your
mother's womb and you are fearfully and wonderfully
made"
I know I been changed!

LOVE

And we have known and believed the love that God hath to us. God is love; and he that dwelleth in love dwelleth in God, and God in him. 1 John 4:16

My first love

My first love is You
My wish of being madly in love with someone came true

You have always been my first love
I just didn't know it
You knew me from the start
And through your love you showed it

You gave me my first kiss
And gave me a life filled with bliss

You wiped away my first tear
And quickly took away my first fear

You were the first person to see me
Before I entered into my mother's womb

You gave me my first gift
You
I accepted that gift
Now my life is free
Thank you Jesus for being the first person to ever die for me!
May 21, 2010

Romans 5:6-8

For when we were yet without strength, in due time Christ died for the ungodly. For scarcely for a righteous man will one die: yet perhaps for a good man some would even dare to die. But God commend his love toward us, in that, while we were yet sinners Christ died for us.

I can't get enough

I can't get enough of your love
I can't get enough of your peace
I can't get enough of your kisses
I can't get enough of your joy
I can't get enough of you
I can't get enough of your word
I can't get enough of your power

I want more of you
If you ever leave me I will die
Nothing will fill this void I have inside
I'm sick of things and stuff
I want more of you Jesus because I can't get enough!

Amazing Grace

When I think of the cross and what it did for me
My mind goes back and I envision a time
When I wasn't free
I was bond by sin
I never thought that I could win
But grace

When I think of the cross and what it did for me
I envision all the suffering, pain, and misery
I never thought anyone would love me
But grace

When I think of the cross and what it did for me
I envision all of the victories that were won for me
By grace

When I think of the cross and what it did for me
Tears roll down my face
When I envision all of Jesus love and grace!
I know that I didn't labor for any of it
Jesus did all the work
He covered all of my sins
And took my place

And this is why
I thank you Jesus
For Your amazing grace!

Romans 3:23 & 24

For all have sinned, and come short of the glory of God;

Being justified freely by his grace through the redemption that is Christ Jesus:

Oh how I love thee

Oh how I love thee
Because You first love me
You made away out of darkness and now I love thee

Oh how I love thee
When I was depress and lonely
You made away for me
You delivered me from my misery

Oh how I love thee
You healed and protected me
You freed me from the hands of the enemy

Oh how I love thee
You gave me a reason to live and to be all the things that
You had ordain for me

Oh how I love thee
You forgave all of my sins and covered me
You are so good to me

Oh how I love thee

Why do you love me?

I sit here with tears in my eyes and I want to know Jesus
why do you love me?

I lied to you

I cursed you

I broke your heart

I turned my back on you

I crucified you

I spit in your face

I didn't trust you

I denied you

I cheated on you

I stole from you

I broke your commandments

After all of that you still love me.

"Because love never fails Rhonda"

*Ephesians 2:4 & 5 But God, who is rich in
mercy, for great love wherewith he loved us.
Even when we were dead in sins, hath quickened
us together with Christ, (by grace ye are saved;)*

We sometimes put God in a box. We draw on our conclusion, what God is supposed to act like and think like. All of us have to realize God isn't like us (man) and God doesn't think like us. He is so above us! It's sad because so many people aren't enjoying a true intimate relationship with Jesus. Some people are scared, angry, disappointed and don't believe. For years I thought God was angry at me. I felt like I had failed Him, and I had to suffer or make God love me. The bottom line is we can't make God love us. He is love! He loves us when we're good and He loves us when we're bad. He hates sin! But He loves His people, and we are made in His image. God wants us to feel and see His love. God wants to show Himself to us. Jesus died so we could have an intimate relationship with our Father God. Yes I had to learn it the hard way but I'm glad I learned. I don't regret any of my past failures or past hurts. They all opened my eyes. I remember a person told me "Rhonda you never stop". I may have got knocked down a lot but Jesus always gave me the power to brush myself off again and get back up! I truly don't believe I would be living this life filled with joy and peace if I didn't have trouble in my life. Trouble made me run to Jesus. The sweet and wonderful thing is Jesus was waiting for me. I ran to Jesus with all of my baggage, addictions, strongholds, soul ties, lies, and drama. Jesus carried all that junk for me. Many times my baggage tried to come back, I immediately took it back to the cross and laid it at the feet of Jesus. The Holy Spirit told me that Jesus died for everything, and excepting Jesus as my Lord and Savior. I wouldn't have to suffer with a life full of sin." The Lord said, "I was Free"! I cried, danced, and screamed.

When we're in bondage to sin our bodies learn to adjust and think that it's ok. Jesus doesn't want us to be comfortable in sin; Jesus wants us to overcome sin in our life through Him! Through Jesus I endured a bad marriage, addictions, angry, low self-esteem and the list goes on!

One thing I realize I'm not God. I'm Rhonda and instead of trying to fight spiritual battles in my own strength I give them to Jesus. I abide in His presence. I love Him so much that I want to please Him. So I study my Bible and learn more about my Father God. Everyday I have to pray and ask God to give me the strength not to sin against Him. I want to bring glory to His name. I want to make Him smile and laugh. Yes, I do believe God smiles and laughs. I want to bring Him joy because He has done so much for me. Jesus set me free from drugs, lust, and gluttony and I'm so grateful. I was on my way to Hell and Jesus step in and said not this time, "I'm going to use Rhonda."

God had to take me to the other side of the mountain in the wilderness. He cleaned me up and purged me from every idol that I had made god in my life. He stripped away pride, anger, and confusion. He took me through test after test. Sometimes He talked me through them then other times He was silent. God knew my life was a mess and He knew that I would one day write a book and give Him all the glory. I can't give anybody else credit for my healing and restoration but Jesus. I'm going to keep telling everybody that Jesus is a healer, deliverer, way maker, friend, joy, peace, love, and

He is everything we will ever need. If you don't believe me then try Him for yourself!

Be careful for nothing; but in everything by prayer and supplication with thanksgiving let your requests be made known unto God.

And the peace of God, which passes all understanding, shall keep your hearts and minds through Christ Jesus. Philippians 4: 6 & 7

Aunt's Love

As I watch you grow into fine adults

I wonder will you remember Aunt's love

I wonder if you remember when I use to play with you

My heart would melt each time I heard you call my
name

My eyes would water whenever I heard your cry

I loved waking up to your beautiful faces

I would do anything for you

You're my nieces and nephews and I will love you all
forever

This is from Aunt with Love

Aunt's love pt. 2

My babies! My loves! My hearts! My sister might have given birth to my nieces and nephews but I still call them my babies. There is nothing like an aunt's love. At the time I wrote this poem I wasn't a mother. I only knew what it felt like to love my sister kids. I can't really describe the feeling all I can say is love! Love! Love! My nieces and nephews play a major role in my life. They're the most beautiful people on the earth! And might I say they love their Aunt Loop. Children are a gift from God. I love my babies. I don't care how old they get I still will call them my babies!

My babies

You are my babies make no mistakes

God made you in his image so you are great

I know life gets hard sometimes

Never give up remember what your made of you have power from Jesus Christ living within so you can change every situation

And start over again

Don't listen to those negative people

You are loved, you are special and you're going to make it

Forget about the past

Keep your head up you are smart, you are strong

You will achieve the destiny that God has ordained for you to receive!

Dedicated to all of my nieces and nephews, I truly do love you all so much.

For You formed my inward parts; You covered me in my mother's womb. I will praise You, for I am fearfully and wonderfully made; Marvelous are Your works. Psalm 139 13:13 & 14

I thank God that we're all made in the image of Christ Jesus. God loves each and every one of us. God has a purpose and destiny for all of us. Yes it will get hard sometimes but we have to trust and believe in Jesus. I thank God for covering my nieces and nephews in there mother's womb. I'm so bless to have great brothers and sisters and adorable and loveable nieces and nephews! Yes! Marvelous are Your works oh God!

My Carmen

You are my ocean, my sky, and my river
You're in my dreams

You are my smile, my laugh, my joy
You're in my mind

You are my friend, my buddy, and my niece
You're in my heart

You are my world, my universe, and my galaxy
You're in my life

You are my moon, my stars, and my sun
You're in my thoughts

You are my hero, my winner, my champion
You're in my head

You are my air, my wind and my breeze
You're truly an angel Ms. Carmen Reeves

Dedicated to my niece 12-20-01

B day poem for Jada

Jada

My love for you is so great
I thank God for this special date November 10th

God used me to give you life and in turn you gave me so
much more

Through you I have learned to love
I thank God above
For giving me a chance to experience motherhood
It haven't been easy but it's all good

Today I shall remember the 9 months I carried you
And the day we were finally joined together
This is a day I will remember forever

Psalm 127:3

*Lo, children are an heritage of the Lord: and the fruit
of the womb is his reward.*

I love my baby

I love you baby Jada

My heart beats for you

You just don't know how your love helped mommy get through

I love you baby Jada

I'm a better person because of you

You just don't know how your love helped mommy get through

I love you baby Jada

I'm glad God sent me you

You just don't know how your love helped mommy get through

Your love made my life better

I promise to love you forever

I love you Jada!

Roses are red
Violets are blue
You are my daughter
And I love you!

My Love bug

You are beautiful

You are wonderful

You are me a tiny, tiny essence of me your mother

I still can't believe me a mother

I was only 25 when you drop into my womb

Confuse, happy, sad, excited, hopeless, and courageous

I was ready

But not really ready

I know that doesn't make sense

No it does make sense

You make sense baby

It made so much sense to me

Watching you grow everyday

You went from crying to mom to mommy

I'm so proud of you

I love the person that you have become

I kiss your every word

Four years old with so much wisdom

You are a breathe of fresh love

Blowing on a summer day

You give me love that tasty like soft chocolate chip
cookies and that smell like fresh ripe strawberries and
that feel like warm water running through my hair

How was I able to be your mother?
I'm honored to know you
I'm honored to be in your presence
I think the world of you
Beautiful you are soft brown coco skin
Beautiful smile
I see love in your almond shapes eyes
Your kisses melt my heart.

Wow I'm a mother! That's what I thought most of Jada's life.

I found out I was pregnant with Jada on my birthday and even though I was in my late twenties, I was still scared and confused. I had lived in Atlanta for almost seven years and now I was pregnant. I called all my friends. And most of friends told me to get an abortion. So I could still go to the clubs and smoke weed. My friends and I made drinking, smoking, and partying our life. And having children was out of the question!

I will never forget the phone conversation I had with my mom. She had called to wish me happy birthday and I sounded so sad. She was like what's wrong I told her I was pregnant. She sounded happy. I quickly told her that I wasn't going to keep the baby. I explained to her that I had my own place, my own job, a new car, and I didn't want a baby. I wasn't saved at the time. I was so selfish, conceded, and foolish. My mother told me to just give the baby up for adoption. Days after our conversation I started having dreams about dead babies and it freaked me out. I didn't know what was going on. My mother told me later that she prayed that God would change my mind.

On my first doctor visit I saw this tiny thing in my body that looked like a finger nail and it had a heart beat it was Jada. The doctor asked me if I would keep the child I said "no". I call the abortion clinic and they told me that the doctor had to give me a due date. I called my doctor and when he gave me my delivery date that's when I knew I couldn't do it. I didn't want to think about what my child would have looked like or what she would have become.

My biggest fear was becoming a single parent, because I saw how my mother suffered. Not having a father around really affected my life for good and bad. I didn't want my daughter to go through that. So I worked two jobs while I was pregnant I had my corporate job at the Equitable in the morning then I caught Marta to Five points to the Gap and worked there in the afternoons.

Pregnant life wasn't so bad, I still wasn't serving the Lord and I stopped going to church because I didn't want people to talk about me. I would read Proverbs to Jada while she was in my womb. One day I made a vow to God if He would allow Jada to be wise and smart, then I told Him I would raise Jada to fear and serve Him. When I had my daughter in 2002 I named her Jada which I later learned it meant wise. I didn't know that at the time. Years had gone by and I forgot about the vow I had made to God. I had Jada in a Christian school and everybody was telling me how smart she was. I was thinking yeah too smart! It's sad but my daughter knew the whole Black album by Jay Z. I had started back smoking weed, clubbing, and drinking like never before. I was a new mom no family, single parent in Atlanta I was stressed almost everyday. My daughter saw me go through a lot; at times she would even wipe away my tears from my face. She was my little angel. I was in my bathroom when the Lord reminded me of the vow that I had made to Him. I knew I had to change I didn't want my daughter to end up like me. God knew I needed to slow down I was on a horrible road heading straight to

Hell. I had some near death experiences and it was only by God's grace that I walked away alive. The devil tried to use my friends to make me terminate my destiny.

Secondly, I had Jada out of wedlock and I repented to God. I should have waited until I was married to have Jada. It's not God's will for us to have children out of wedlock, and He doesn't want us to have sex before marriage. It's also not God's will for us to masturbate or have sex with the same sex, all of it is sin and it will eventually end with death! If we don't truly repent and allow Jesus to change us, then we will die in our sins. I thank Jesus for delivering me from having sex outside of marriage. The wages of sin is death. I always tell my daughter for every action there is consequence. For every bad action there is a bad consequence and for every good action there is a good consequence. I was having sex outside of marriage and I was dying in my own sin that was my consequence. I thank God that I repented and ask forgiveness. He has forgiven me for my sins.

Lastly, if you're having sex outside of marriage then you need to ask God to help you stop. You can't stop on your own. Jesus died on the cross and rose again for all of our sins. I don't care how many sex partners or abortions you have had Jesus will forgive you. You have to truly repent. I look up the word repent in the Webster's dictionary and repent means: To feel regret for something which has occurred; to change one's sinful way. You have to turn away from sin or you will die in your sin. Yes we do serve a God that will turn any situation around for our good. But if you refuse to truly repent and turn from your sin then you will die and go to hell. God's word says "Everything is permissible for me but not everything is beneficial. Everything is permissible for me, but I will not be mastered by anything. Food for the stomach and the stomach for food, but God will destroy them both. The body is not meant for sexual immortality, but for the Lord, and the Lord for the body. By His power God raised the Lord from the dead, and He will raise us also. Do you not know that your bodies are members of Christ and unite them with a prostitute? Never! Do you not know that he who united himself with a prostitute is one with her in body? For it is said, "the two will become one flesh". But he who unites himself with the Lord is one with him in spirit. Flee from sexual immorality. All other sins a man commits are outside his body, but he who sins sexually sins against his own body. Do you not know that your body is a temple of the Holy Spirit, who is in you, whom you have received from God? You are not your own; you were brought at a price. Therefore honor God with your body. 1 Corinthians 6:12-20".

Furthermore, I joined my body to a lot of people just like the scripture said in 1 Corinthians and the Holy Spirit showed me the reason why Low Self-Esteem! I couldn't believe that I had low self-esteem, because I really thought I was cute. I used clothes, hair weaves, makeup, sex, and drugs to make me feel special. And as long as I had those things in my life then I felt cute. I didn't know that I was a child of The Most God with a destiny and a purpose over my life. And I had no idea that my body belonged to the Lord and not me. I didn't have a relationship with my Father God so I lowered my standards and had sex with guys I didn't liked nor loved it was just something to do. I didn't love myself so I couldn't love another person. I suffered with rejection. I wanted so badly to be loved that I took sex for love. I allowed guys to treat me any kind of way just so I could feel loved and accepted. Now don't feel sorry for me because I mistreated a lot of guys and I'm so sorry for it. I asked God to forgive me for all the men I hurt and I turned from my sins. I realized hurt people hurt other people.

When we thirst after something bad enough we will do anything to get it. We will steal, kill, lie, and cheat just so someone can love and accept us. God had to deliver me from people. Jesus love and accepts me so I don't care what people say or do to me because Jesus is the Lover of my soul. I don't need sex or a man for love. God is love and now that I have a relationship with Jesus guess what I have love! I can give love to other people. I leave you with these scriptures: Matthew 22: 37-39, Jesus replied: "Love the Lord your God with all your heart and with all your soul and with all your mind. This is the first and greatest commandment. And second is like it: Love your neighbor as yourself." Be Bless!

Beautiful

You are beautiful and unique
Strong and wise
And all so sweet

You are love and peace
Gentle and humble
You mean so much to me

You are my love and my sister
Bold and smart
You will always have a place in my heart
You are me and I'm you
You are beautiful

Dedicated to Genia M.

Proverbs 31:10
Who can find a virtuous woman for her price is far above
rubies.

Proverbs 17:17 says "a friend loveth at all times. And that is so true of you Genia, even though I didn't keep my end of the deal. Sorry! I have never had a friend like you. I longed and hoped for a true friend like you Genia.

It was in the summer time in Atlanta Georgia and I went to Mega fest at the Georgia Dome, not knowing that my life would be changed forever! People were every where, I couldn't believe my eyes. I just wanted to see Juanita Bynum. I had her book and my bible. Once Juanita finished speaking a gentleman said that Juanita Bynum would be signing book and cds. I immediately left to find Juanita and be the first person in line. One problem I couldn't find the line nor could anyone else. I asked so many people and they all gave me the wrong directions. Until I came across this young lady she was very nice and she was giving away free coupons for bleach. She asked me if I wanted one and I told her no. I explained to her that I was looking for Juanita Bynum. This nice young lady gave me the correct directions. I thanked her and took some coupons. By the time I got there the line was long and I was a little upset.

Once in line I started talking to some young ladies in front of me and we shared our testimonies of pain, betrayal, and our victories. I didn't know that someone was listening and taking all of it in. Eugenia Moss was standing behind me. She joined in our conversation and we talked for a long time. The next thing I knew we were standing face to face with Juanita Bynum. I handed her my book, she signed it. I looked back at Genia and she was crying. Everybody went their separate ways except Genia and I. We went and had lunch and talked, we exchanged phone numbers and it was an immediate connection between us.

Months went by and trouble came knocking hard at my door. I was in a very bad state and I remember getting a message on my cell phone and it went something like this: I been thinking about you and praying for you I love you and it will get better. It was Genia. I couldn't believe it, I was feeling so bad and God used her message to give me hope. I called her back and we talked for hours and hours. I felt so much better. Proverbs 27:17 says "Iron sharpeneth iron; so a man sharpeneth the countenance of his friend."

Years have gone by, and by God's grace we are still best friends. God has used Genia, to teach me how to love and be in a friendship. I never respected anybody, I just wanted my way. And once Genia realized that she had to put her foot down. I never really had anyone stand up to me so I tried to walk away from our friendship but Genia keep coming back no matter how mean or cruel I was to her. She loved me with the love of Christ. Genia saw something in me that I couldn't see in myself. Thank you Genia for never giving up on me or on our friendship, I truly do cherish you.

Nobody knows me like Genia. You can ask Genia anything about me and she knows it. I'm laughing now! Genia and I have two things in common Jesus and ice cream! Just like Jesus died on the cross for us. A part of me had to die for Genia. I couldn't just treat her any kind of way. I had to die to my selfish needs and think about her feelings. And it was so hard! And just like the sweet taste of ice cream our friendship gets sweet and sweet every day. I have learned the most important keys to friendship are Jesus, servant hood, honesty, and love. I have made a sound decision to love Genia no matter what we go through. I have also chosen to serve her and be honest with her. Genia will say sometimes I'm too honest! Its ok Jesus isn't finish with me yet! Genia and I have put Jesus first in our life. Jesus is the source of our friendship. Jesus brought us together and He will keep us together until eternality! Genia and I are Jesus girls for life.

You have truly been a blessing to me Genia. I thank God for you.

I love you Eugenia Moss!

Daddy

I look for you

Your not there

Tell me how I should feel, longing to have you near

I try to imagine you

Holding me and keeping me away from harm

It's sad when I can't find you by my side

I wish that you could show me a sign of your love and affection so I would know that your feelings are real

I find myself feeling abandon and neglected

I'm a part of you and it's time you accept it

Look at my features

They came from you

Even my attitude

Being a so-called strong black man

I'm sure you know what to do

It hurts so bad that I could cry

My daddy

The years have come and went

So there's really no need to bother

You were out of sight

But never out of mind

I wish that we could reunite

I feel that it's time to make things right

I forgive you for all the times
You weren't there
I hope we can start over
Because I will always care for my
Daddy! 9/21/1997

At one point in my life I hated my father, I expected so much out of him and he never delivered. And I allowed the pain to build up over months and years. I was young and I really didn't understand how could you make a child and not be in their life. I realized anybody can make a baby but only a man can be a father. It's so sad!

Once I got older and learned more about my dad. I found out that his father wasn't around and he was the oldest child, so he had to grow up fast and be the father to his brothers and sisters. He dropped out of school and got a job. As I sat down and talk to my father about his life I could hear the hurt in his voice and for once I could feel his pain. Nobody taught my dad how to be a good father. He never got to see that father daughter or father son relationship. I believe deep down inside my daddy was crying and searching for love. It's so sad because we as a society teach little boys not to cry so they grow up mad at the world, hating everybody. Then we expect for them to become loving fathers! My father cried out for love through drugs, sex, and alcohol. He had a void in his heart that only God could fill and he never had a personal relationship with Jesus. My dad decided to fill that void with anything. It's sad, because I'm a lot like my dad. I did exactly what my dad did, I didn't have a father so I look to people and things to give me love that only my Heavenly Father could give me.

In the summer of 2007, when I was at my lowest of lows, I went to visit my father. I sat down with my dad and told him how I felt about him. I told him that I had hatred in my heart towards him. I told him how I tried to make every man in my life pay for what my daddy did and didn't do. I told him I treated men like dirt. I told him how I really hated men. Once I told my daddy everything then I apologized to him and once I apologizing to him I was now able to apologize to all the men I had hurt. I realized my dad couldn't be a father if nobody ever showed him how to be one. You can't give away what you don't have.

On that Sunday afternoon, I fell in love with my daddy. God healed my heart that day. I explained to my dad, that even though he wasn't there for me I did have a loving father Jesus and He gave me love when my dad wasn't there. I told my daddy that I had forgiven him and I asked him to forgive me and he did. I learned that I had a lot of my daddy's bad and good habits. Before I left my dad's house, he told me that he loved me and that he had a wonderful time with me. My heart jumped inside of me and I smiled and told my dad I love him and God bless him.

Lastly, just like I had to be honest with my earthly dad, I had to also be honest with my heavenly Father God. I had to tell Him about all my pain, hurt and rejection. I had to be real with Him. I learned a valuable lesson that day Proverbs 10:12 love covers all sins. Be bless!

My Pastor

You're a gift, you're a dream, and your life is extraordinary never secondary. You have lived a life that is legendary.

You're a pastor you're a husband and you have given your time, life, hopes and dreams to building up God's teams.

You're a fighter, you're a winner you never settle for less, you are always here serving and doing your best.

You're a warrior; you're a shepherd covering God's people treating all of us as equal.

You're a dad, a friend; you have a heart for God's people
You are a light of God's glory shining brighter and faster
Thank you Jesus for my amazing pastor

Dedicated to my Pastor Waid Hobbs

I want more

I want more of your love
When I feel unloved

I want more of your peace
When I feel stress

I want more of your wisdom
When I feel confuse

I want more of your strength
When I feel weak

I want more of your glory
When I feel useless

I want more of your joy
When I feel depress

I want more of your presence
When I feel alone

The truth is Jesus I want all of you. I want to live, breath, and
sleep you. You can call me a Jesus Freak, but all I know is
when I needed a friend Jesus was there. When I needed love
He loved me. When I needed healing Jesus healed me. And for
that I can't get enough I want more of Jesus

COMPLETE

And ye are complete in Him,
which is the head of all
principality and power.
Colossians 2:10

Smile

You are my all
I truly do love you

Thank you for opening my eyes and heart to you
I know the real meaning of agape love

Because of you I'm free to love
You're my friend, my love, my heart, my world

You are my everything
I love you. I love you

I think of you and I smile
I talk to you and I smile

I sing to you and I smile
I cry out to you and I smile

You make me smile Jesus

Complete

Young women take back your wisdom
Young men take back your strength

Mother take back your love
Daddy take back your peace

Sister take back your freedom
Brother take back your power

Young women take back your education
Young men take back your authority

Mother take back your family
Daddy take back your children

Sister take back your dreams
Brother take back your visions

Jesus paid the price so we could take back everything
that belongs to us.

Dedicated to Prophetess Mattie Nottage

I came to give

I came to give love to the hurting
I came to give strength to the weak
I came to give victory to the defeated
I came to give hope to the hopeless
I came to give joy to the depress
I came to give deliverance to the bondage
I came to give wisdom to the foolish
I came to give healing to the sick
I came to give peace to the restless
I came to give life to the dying
I came to give you Jesus!

In YOU I Live!
Outside of You I'm nothing!

You are my expression to live
In You I live

In You I have unspeakable joy
My life is beautiful now that I have You

You wake me up every morning with a fresh kiss of life
You give me life

In You I live

My afternoons are filled with thoughts of You
I sneak away privately to tell You I love You

I don't need a cell phone to call or text You
You are always near to me Your Spirit lives within
me

No eye contact needed to be made You just tug at me
heart
So I give You all my time

Loving You stays on my mind
See I want more than ever to please You

I want to bless You with my lips
And adore You with my behavior

Yes I know You're always watching me
So I make sure my heart is right towards You and
Your people

Because I know You love us all equal
By evening time I'm anxious to get alone with
You
So I can discuss my day to You

You always listen even when I sometimes feel like You
don't
You always assure me not to go by feelings
because feelings change

You have given me a promise and I know Your word is
true
So I close my eyes and rest in You

Your grace and love overflows me
Sometimes I cry because You're so good to me

I even wonder why You love being with me
You say "because You made me, my dear"

Yes Your right I'm made in Your image
You knew me before anybody knew me

You know what I like
I'm so glad I know what true love is

I'm so grateful that in You I live!

Acts 17:28 For in Him we live, and move, and have our being;

I know you're probably thinking what in the world is wrong with her! I'm totally head over hills in love with Jesus Christ. I'm not ashamed to tell the world how I feel about my Savior, my Daddy, my Best Friend, my Husband, my Rock, my One Desire!! I suffered for so long with rejection and depression. I was rejected by strangers but what hurt the most, was that I was rejected by people I loved. My rejection turned to depression then the suicidal thoughts came then the suicidal attempts. I'm so grateful God didn't let me die. I would have never known how much Jesus truly loved me. I never thought I could ever be loved like this. The amazing thing is Jesus love never stops. God's word says "Jesus will never leave nor forsake me". No matter what I do! I don't have to earn His love. And because I know Jesus loves and approves of me. I'm now able to love other people even if they choose not to love me back. I care so much about Jesus that I will do anything to please Him. For example writing this book is to please and glorify him.

Wow! My life is now complete because I have the kind of love I always wanted. This agape love didn't come from a car, house, job, money, a man, drugs, or a child. This love came from Jesus my true source for life. I realize everybody wants to be loved and accepted. We are made to want love and acceptance but so many times we mistake lust for love. I had a very bad lust problem I would lust over food, clothes, and men. Things get old and lust will fade away. The Bible says "God is love". God's love is eternal. We should never put all of our trust in things and people. One thing I learned in my 33 years of living is that things and people will fail you!

Jesus love is perfect. God's word says "Blessed is the man who makes the Lord his trust and does not respect the proud nor such as turn aside to lies". Please don't fall for the lie (The American Dream) it's just that, a dream! You can have the nicest house, most expensive car, a beautiful spouse, but if you don't have a relationship with Jesus then you have nothing. Jesus isn't a myth or a dream. Jesus is the truth and the way to eternal life. There is no other path! Jesus is the only door to our Father God and true salvation. Yes it may sound too good to be true but believe me it's true. All you have to do is confess Jesus as Lord and the Son of the true living God. You must ask Jesus to forgive you of your sins. Then ask Him to come into your heart and change you. Believe in your heart that He is the Son of the living God. Your life will never be the same. Well, you can write a tell-all book. I don't know but one thing I do know is that with God your life will never be the same. It is a life that is forever changed!

I love you!

I love to love you Jesus
I love to sing praises to your name
I love to adore you
I love to honor you
I love to talk to you
I love to just be in your presence
I love to love you Lord
God is love
Jesus you make my life so complete
You fill me up with you goodness
You give me peace and joy
Lord I thank you so much
You're my every thing
You're my life and my strength
Please keep taking me deeper in you
I need and want more of you Jesus

I need YOU!

I need You so bad it hurts
I need to feel Your touch
I need to hear Your voice
I need to see You
I need to be around You
I need to hide and rest in You
I need You

I need to love You
I need to be real with You
I need to tell You the truth
I need to show You love
I need to trust You
I need to surrender to You
I need to receive You
I need to worship You
I need You

I need to sing to You
I need to write love letters to You
I need to make You first in my life
I need to draw near to You
I need to honor You

I need You

I need to tell people about You
I need to talk about You
I need to show people You
I need to write a book about You
I need You

I need You in my school
I need You in my life
I need You in my home
I need You in my car
I need You in my heart
I need You in my daughter's life
I need You in my church
I need You in my marriage
I need You in my book
I need You

I need to tell You that You are faithful
I need to tell You that You are holy
I need to tell, You are the Son of the living God
I need to tell You that there is no other god like You
I need to tell You that You are the true living God
I need to tell You that You are Jesus Christ

I need to tell You that You are the Alpha and Omega
I need to tell You that You are my God
I need to tell You I love You
I need You

I need to end this poem or I will be writing forever. The bottom line is I need You Jesus! The world needs Jesus!

Dedicated to Tommy Tenney

Thank you, for writing God Chasers and God Catchers, your books have changed my life forever!

Life that is poured out

You can't pour anything into something that's already full. The question today what are you full of?

I want to live a life poured out
A life poured out for Jesus

I want God to empty me of every evil thought, evil desire and man made tradition
I want to live a life poured out

I want to pour out God's grace, love, and mercy all over the place
I want God to empty me of my hopes, goals, and dreams

I want to pour out God's goodness and His glory on all of you
I want to live a life poured out for Jesus

I want God to empty me from every sin and addiction
And fill me with self-control and power

I want to pour out God's forgiveness and compassion on all of you

See I'm sick of filling up on people and material things, stuff that won't last

I need eternal stuff that will help me past every test and trial the enemy throw my way

And help me fulfill God's destiny.

Please Father God empty me!

My everything

When I find myself trapped at the end of a tunnel
You are my light

When I find myself beaten up by everyday
struggles
You are my strength

When I find myself broke without a dime
You are my wealth

When I find myself alone and heartbroken
You are my love

When I find myself abandon by family and friends
You are my rock!

Thank you Holy Spirit!

The Mirror

When I look in the mirror what do I see
I see a beautiful person looking at me

When I look in the mirror what do I see
I see a woman that was trap but now is free

When I look in the mirror what do I see
I see a woman that was once enslaved by what people
thought of me

When I look in the mirror what do I see
I see a woman that has love, peace, and joy running all
over me

When I look in the mirror what do I see
I see a child of the Most High God looking at me!

You make me feel

As I look into the mirror I'm a reflection of Your
goodness, grace, mercy, and love
You make me feel Beautiful

As I walk down the street I'm aware of Your love,
power, joy, and presence
You make me feel Adored

As I sit down in my room I know Your touch, words, and
Your embrace
You make me feel Loved

As I write this poem I know You are close to me I feel
Your love, freedom, and deliverance running over me
You make me feel Free

As I rest in You I'm renewed, empowered, blessed, and
healed
Jesus Christ I love the way You make me feel!

You are my Rock

As I sit here writing this poem
The only thing on my mind is You Lord
My rock

See You are my rock, my life, my dreams, my hope
Your love keeps me afloat

So many people and things try to tear me down
People leave deals fall through
But You Lord
You always see me through

See You are my rock, my world, my love, my peace
Your love helps me release
Myself from all negative
So what with my past I'm moving forward
And this time life will be a blast
I have my rock to lead on

See You are my everything
I have all things in You
I no longer live a life in quick sand
I had to get off the wrong block

I have a new desire that keeps my heart on fire

His name is Jesus and my love for Him will never stop
Because He is my rock.

You are my life

My life belongs to You

You are my life Lord!

I have no being without You

I need You to live, to be, to love, to think, to move, to laugh

I need You everyday, every hour, every minute, and every second

My life is nothing without You

Life means nothing to me if I can't have You Jesus

You are my world, my strength, my joy, my peace

You are my life Jesus!

I'm still here

Proverbs 24:10 If thou faint in the day of adversity, thy strength is small.

Through all the tears
I'm still here
Through custody battles
I'm still here
Through heartaches
I'm still here
Through all the lies
I'm still here
Through every fight
I'm still here
Through all the pain
I'm still here
Through broken relationships
I'm still here
Through sickness
I'm still here
Through every car accident
I'm still here
Through death
I'm still here
Through divorce

I'm still here

You tried to kill me
I'm still here
You tried slander my name
I'm still here
You tried to tear me down
I'm still here
You tried to destroy me
I'm still here
You tried to kill my dreams
I'm still here
You tried to steal my mind
I'm still here
You tried to take my ministry
I'm still here
You tried to take my daughter
I'm still here
You tried to stop me from writing this book
I'm still here

You left me
I'm still here
You broke my heart
I'm still here

You told me I was ugly

I'm still here

You told me that I would never be anything

I'm still here

You beat on me

I'm still here

You took my marriage

I'm still here

You lied on me

I'm still here

You molested me

I'm still here

You took my house

I'm still here

You took my car

I'm still here

You took my job

I'm still here

You should have killed me when you had the chance!

But I'm still here!

Luke 10:19 Behold, I give unto you power to tread on serpents and scorpions, and over all the power of the enemy: and nothing shall by any means hurt you.

Dedicated to Dr. Juanita Bynum

I'm still here in my anthem, it's my life story. I realized why my life was so rough God had a purpose for me. I was an underdog most of my life. I was the baby in my family. I had an older brother and sister. They taught me how to be tough. I learned to fight my way out of situations and I took that same mindset into my adulthood. I remember winning and losing some fights, it was ok I was just glad to be alive to talk about it.

I'm really into football and for some reason I love to cheer for the underdogs. I guess that's what makes a good story and a football game. It's always fun to see a team come back from being behind and win a game. And in football you have your team and you have the enemy! The enemy's team main goal is to defeat the other team and make them go home with their tail between their legs. There have been times when my team lost the game and of course I was upset. The bottom line is we as human beings hate to lose!

My life has been much like a football game and each year just like football I have went through different seasons in my life. The enemy has tried to use different tricks from his playbook. Most football players learn from their mistakes. I realized the more time I spent with my coach (Jesus) the better I became and as long as I listen to my quarterback the (Holy Spirit) I was o.k. The bottom line is we're all after the Super bowl trophy. Paul said in Philippians 3:14 I press toward the mark for the prize of the high calling of God in Christ Jesus. I had to press my way through every test, trial, and heartache. I had to overcome, just like Jesus did on the cross. He overcame the beatings, persecutions, jealous, and all the lies. But one thing about Jesus He never sin. He was crucified for our sins. Jesus was blameless. He never sin against God. And Jesus reward was eternal life and a wonderful seat in Heaven with God plus souls for God's kingdom! I have sin against God and God's people. And it all came back around. The pain that I put people through was the same pain I got back and double! The bible says in Galatians 6:7&8 do not be deceived: God cannot be mocked. A man reaps what he sows. The one who sows to please his sinful nature, from that nature will reap destruction; the one who sows to please the Spirit, from the Spirit will reap eternal life. Most of my life I sowed to my sinful nature. I was on the enemy (devil) team. I followed the devil's playbook. I did things to people that I regret. And I thought once I repented and asked Jesus into my heart that everything would be great. God did forgive me of my sins, but I still had to reap a harvest from the bad seeds that I sown in my past. I praise God because yes I cried a lot and yes it hurt but God gave me the power to get through it all. And now that I have learned my lesson on seed, time, and harvest. I make a point to only sow seeds of love, kindness, patience, peace, and honesty. I no longer have to lie and cheat to get my way. I trust God for all I need. Sometimes it gets hard, because I have to sow love, peace, and honesty to my enemies. Galatians 6:9 and let us not be weary in well doing: for in due season we shall reap. If we faint not. And my due season is here praise God! My super bowl trophy is this book and all the millions of soul that are being saved, delivered, and set free by the blood of Jesus. The Bible says in Revelation 12:11 "and they overcame him (the devil) by the blood of the Lamb (Jesus), and by the word of their testimony."

And like football, after every game the winning team comes out and talks about the game and they share how they defeated the enemy's team, it's called a press conference. This book is my press conference!

First and foremost we have to know which team we're on Mark 3:23-26 says "how can satan drive out satan? If a kingdom is divided against itself, that kingdom cannot stand. If a house is divided against itself, that house cannot stand. And if satan opposes himself and is divided he cannot stand". I tried to be on the devil's team and God's team. A player in football can't be on two teams at the same time and it's like that in real life. I couldn't serve both so I had to choose. Revelation 3:15 says I know your deeds, that you are neither cold nor hot. I wish you were either one or the other! So, because you are lukewarm-neither hot nor cold-I am about to spit you out of my mouth. And that is exactly what happened to me. I was attending church and still smoking weed. I had to make a decision life or death either Jesus or the devil. I switch to Jesus team and I immediately became a winner. Because it wasn't me doing all the work it was Jesus working through me. Jesus gave me the power to overcome every obstacle that the devil threw my way. The devil had a lot of trick plays! He tried to kill me so many times. The devil was mad because I switch teams in the middle of the season. And in football when a player switches teams, people get mad! I didn't care I just wanted to be on the winning team and I'm now an over comer! I leave you these scriptures Romans 8:37&38 Nay, in all these things we are more than conquerors through him that loved us. For I am persuaded that neither death, nor life, nor angels, nor principalities, nor power, nor things present, nor things to come, nor height, nor depth, nor any other creature shall be able to separate us from the love of God which is in Christ Jesus our Lord. God bless!

My Happy Ending

And they lived happily ever after!
Is it really true?

I gave 20 of my good years to a job and still got fired
I stayed faithful to a marriage for years and it ended
I took my child to church every Sunday and they still got
on drugs
I ate healthy and exercise; I still got sick
I hired the best lawyer for my trial and they still sent me
to jail
I told the truth and I still got blamed for the crime
I put my trust in a person and they still betrayed me
I realize true happiness wasn't a matter of material things
And what I do
My true happiness is found in You
Jesus!

God never promise us a life without trouble. But His grace! Sometimes God will allow us to go through tough times to make us better and more dependent on Him. Jesus wants to be our source for love, peace, happiness, and joy. When you ask most people what makes them happy or bring them joy. Most people will say my job, my children, my house, my car, my money, my drugs, my marriage, and my jewelry. Not too many people will say Jesus. And for a long time I never said Jesus, I thought joy and happiness came from material things. And if I was having a good day then I was happy and if I was having a bad day then I was unhappy. But once I allowed Jesus into my heart; Jesus fill me with joy. I learned how to find peace and joy in Jesus and not in my situation. Joy isn't a job, marriage, house, or a person. True joy is Jesus and if you don't have a personal relationship with Him then you won't have joy. Anybody can be happy but on Jesus can give you joy unspeakable joy! And the Bible says in Philippians 4:7 "and the peace of God which transcends all understanding will guard your hearts and your minds in Christ Jesus". I looked up the word transcend in the Webster's dictionary and it said to exceed. Jesus gives us joy that exceeds every test, trial, tragedy, pain, and heartache. I remember when my great uncle died and my great grandmother still had joy in the mist of her pain. It was nothing but God's grace. God will give you grace to face those hurtful situations.

Jesus has giving me the power to forgive all of my enemies and move on. Jesus can give you the power to serve a life sentence with peace, knowing that Jesus love is all you need. God has giving me the grace to stay on a job I hated. We have to take our eyes off our problems and look to Jesus for help. We are free in Jesus. I learned if I wanted to live a sanctified life style then I had to ask Jesus to help me. I remember wanting to go deep in God but I didn't know how. And my friend told me to just ask Jesus to give you me a desire for more of Him. I remember feeling bad, I felt like I should have already had a desire for more of God. I realize all of us were born into sin so our bodies naturally desire sin over righteousness. We have to ask Jesus to change our desires and give us His desires. Now Jesus knew no sin and He only desired the will of God. And we should desire the will of God. First we have to ask for help from Jesus. We can't make ourselves holy. We can't deliver ourselves from sin, only Jesus can do that. But when we choose not to ask for help then we end up falling deeper into sin. We get into bondage to sin and it leads to death.

Today whatever you're going through Gods grace will get you through it. Things might not workout the way you wanted it to. And that's ok; just keep your eyes on Jesus!

As I finish this book I'm compel to get naked and uncovered before you. The Lord thought it would be good to end this book with Happily Ever After! Like I told you before, I have been writing this book for over 18 years. And I have seen and been through a lot. In my early childhood and most of my teens, I dealt with depression so bad that I would pray for God to kill me in my sleep. I even tried to overdose. But God's grace! In my twenties I got addicted to weed, had a child out of wedlock, and ended up living in a homeless shelter. But

God's grace! I got married thinking that would solve all of my problems and my husband cheated, left, and had a child out of wedlock during our marriage. But God's grace! My daughter and I got evicted from our apartment and we had to move back to Florida. My sister died leaving behind four beautiful children. My car stopped working. But God's grace! You would look at my life and feel sorry for me. And for many years I felt sorry for myself. I cried, complained and got angry. Then I realize it wasn't even about me. I had a Paul and Jesus moment. In Matthew 26:39 Jesus said "O my Father, if it be possible, let this cup pass me from me: nevertheless not as I will, but as thou will. I made up my mind, if all the stuff in my past didn't kill me. Then I was going to do the will of God no matter what the cost! Every stripe that Jesus took was a stripe for our healing. It cost you something to do the will of God. But God will reward His children. Paul said in Romans 8:18 For I reckon that the suffering of this present time are not worthy to be compared with the glory which shall be revealed in us. I have made a decision to suffer for Jesus. A lot of times I just wanted the blessings. I just want to be saved and go to Heaven. I was tired of fighting. But I realize we have so many people dying in this world from depression, lust, drugs, and a life without Jesus. And God put me here to say no there is another way you don't have to die in sin. You don't have to kill yourself. You don't have to keep having sex outside of marriage. I'm here to say that Jesus Christ changed me and He will do the same for you. I had to survive every test and trial. I realize there is purpose in my pain, yes I did bad things. And yes bad things were done to me. But God grace! I gave God all my issues and pain. And Jesus blood has covered my sins. And Jesus is changing me everyday! Everyday I wake up with new grace and new mercy. I could have died in my pain. But God's grace! I knew at a very young age that God had a purpose for me. That's why the devil attacked me so hard. My great grandmother taught me to call on the name of Jesus. So when I got older I still called on Jesus and in 2005 on Super bowl Sunday in Atlanta in my apartment. Jesus answered my cry and changed me. And my life has never been the same!

So yes, you can live happily ever after with Jesus!

If you have never made Jesus Lord over your life, then now you can. Just say this prayer out loud and believe within your heart. And you will be saved!

Jesus I confess that I'm a sinner. Please forgive me of my sins. I desperately need you. Please help me Jesus. I confess that you are the Son of the true living God. Jesus please come into my heart and save me. I choose this day to make you Lord over my life Jesus. I declare that I am saved! I'm free from sin. I'm yours Jesus I surrender my life to you. Thank you for saving me.

* If you said the sinner's prayer and truly meant it, then praise The Almighty God! Please pray and ask God to help you find a church home. You will need other Christian to help you stay on the right track.

If you need a bible please write to me:

Rhonda Smith

P.O. Box 471

Lake Como Fl, 32157

Or you can email me at: inYouilive7@ hotmail.com or inyouilive.com

Heavenly Father, I pray this prayer in the power of the Holy Spirit, Father God I thank you for saving me. I thank you God for loving me. Thank you for changing me. I need you to help me Jesus. Father God give me a thirst and hungry for you. Father help me to seek your face. I want more of you Jesus. Father God teach me how to pray. Teach me how to love you Jesus. God please give me a meek and humble spirit. Father give me a spirit of boldness and courage to serve you. Remove every spirit of fear, confuse, lust, and lying from me. Father I give my life to you this day. I surrender my family, my children, and my friends to you. I ask you Jesus to move powerfully in my life and my families life. Father take away every ungodly desire and give me your Godly desires. Give me wisdom and revelation of you and your word. Give me a desire to read my bible. Father please send Godly righteous men and women into my life to help me draw closer to you. I declare Lord you will remove every distraction out of my life. Remove anyone in my life that will try to stop me from serving you Jesus. I declare this day that I am a child of God. I declare this day I will submit myself to God and I will resist the devil in the name of Jesus. I declare no weapon formed against me shall prosper. I declare this day that I am a new person in Christ. I take authority over this day in Jesus name. It shall be prosperous for me and I will walk in God's love. Holy Spirit please lead and guide me today. Jesus I want to have an encounter with you like never before. Jesus please make yourself real to me. I love you Jesus. Thank you Jesus. And I believe that you have heard my prayer. I believe that you have answered my prayer. In Jesus name Amen!

Coming Soon!

The audio version of *In You I live* the book.

Plus *In You I live* the album, with singing and spoken word.

Collection of Christian children books.

Please check out my website for dates and prices. www.inyouilive.com

www.ingramcontent.com/pod-product-compliance
Lightning Source LLC
Chambersburg PA
CBHW072013040426
42447CB00009B/1618